Praise for Terence Noonan and Marta Tracy

"Terence and Marta are consummate professionals. They infuse their work with years of useful experience, 'no nonsense' advice, and a great sense of creativity and playfulness."

—Fran Sorin, author of *Digging Deep: Unearthing Your Creative Roots Through Gardening* and gardening expert on DIY Network's *Home Made Easy*

"Terence and Marta gave me inside secrets to presenting myself to the media in a way that emphasizes my strengths and has helped build the Chantecaille brand on TV."

—Olivia Chantecaille, creative director, Chantecaille Cosmetics

"I recommend Marta and Terence to all my clients; their candid advice has proven to be the best direction for anyone looking to get on TV. They are the industry insiders who don't just talk the talk, they have proven techniques."

—Jodi Turk, TurkTV Management

"Terence and Marta are a fountain of creative, tangible ideas and the know-how to get it all done when it comes to using the power of the media. They are the 'real deal' for marketing professionals."

—Tricia Chan, principal and founder, Public Group

About the Authors

TERENCE NOONAN is a four-time Emmy winner and currently a co-executive producer at FOX Television on *The Morning Show with Mike and Juliet*. Previously, he worked at Sony Pictures Television in daytime talk development and for five years he was a producer on *The Rosie O'Donnell Show*. Terence has produced celebrity and lifestyle television for more than a decade and worked with Ellen DeGeneres, Isaac Mizrahi, and many others. He lives in New York City with his partner, Dimitri.

MARTA TRACY is a television executive who created and launched The Style Network as senior vice president of programming. She was one of the original creators of E! Entertainment Television, where she served for ten years as vice president of talent development. Marta has developed content for Matt Lauer, Elizabeth Hasselbeck, and Howard Stern. She now has her own media company where she works with entrepreneurs and businesses for maximum credibility and media exposure to increase brand recognition and generate additional revenue. Brand by brand, she is a catalyst for creating content on television and across multiple media platforms. She works in Manhattan and has a son, Christian, attending college in Los Angeles.

KAREN KELLY is a lifestyle and business writer.

STARRING YOU!

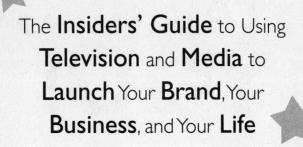

The **Insiders' Guide** to Using **Television** and **Media** to **Launch** Your **Brand**, Your **Business**, and Your **Life**

STARRING YOU!

TERENCE NOONAN
and MARTA TRACY

with Karen Kelly

HARPER ● ENTERTAINMENT

NEW YORK ● LONDON ● TORONTO ● SYDNEY

HARPER ENTERTAINMENT

HarperCollins books may be purchased for educational, business, or sales promotional use. For information please write: Special Markets Department, HarperCollins Publishers, 10 East 53rd Street, New York, NY 10022.

FIRST EDITION

Designed by Joy O'Meara

Library of Congress Cataloging-in-Publication Data is available upon request.

ISBN: 978-0-06-117112-3
ISBN-10: 0-06-117112-3

07 08 09 10 11 ❖/RRD 10 9 8 7 6 5 4 3 2 1

For my partner, Dimitri—you are my sunshine.
And to my sister, Kathleen—we made it through the rain.
—Terence

To my father, who taught me that life gives you
second chances if you open your eyes to see them.
And also to my loving mother, Meta, and my son, Christian,
who both taught me that it is a gift to love and to be loved.
—Marta

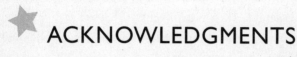 ACKNOWLEDGMENTS

Thank you to our writer, Karen Kelly, who "got" our voice and understood our message from the first meeting, and then translated it beautifully on to the page. We would not have this book without her.

Thanks also go to our agent, Claudia Cross at Sterling Lord Literistic, who found the perfect home for *Starring You!*, and who protected out interests every step of the way.

Jeremy Cesarec, the hippest and smartest editor in town. From the very beginning your ideas and excitement about the book have made you our most important and appreciated cheerleader.

Hope Innelli, our HaperCollins maketing guru, whose vision, creativity, and enthusiam took *Starring You!* to a whole new level.

Special thanks to Melanie Chilek (senior vice president, programming) and Gerrette Allegra (vice president, programming) at Sony Pictures Television for their inspiration during the many times we collaborated together.

To all the incredible media professionals included in the book for sharing their wisdom, insights, and insider secrets. We cannot thank you enough for being part of this project:

Jennifer Aiello, Manette Ansay, Rachel Ashwell, Fred Barnes, Cindi Berger, Bradly Bessey, Lloyd Boston, Cordelia Bowe, Fran Brescia, Jane Buckingham, Tony Burton, Tucker Carlson, Jenn Cohn, Constantine, Julie Cooper, Denise Cramsey, Paula Deen, Alex Duda, David Evangelista, Lash Fary, Bethanny Frankel, Paula Frolich, Raina Seitel Gittlin, Gina Glickman, Nancy Grace, Jon Harris, Mark Itkin, Joanna Jordan, Emily Kaufman, Jim Kozloff, Tara Kraft, Albert Lewitinn, Tara Lowenberg, Debbi Matenopoulis, Allie McKay, Matt Messinger, Amy Metrick Hornstein, Todd Miller, Isaac Mizrahi, Michael Moloney, Linda Oken, Jami Osieki, Nicholas Perricone, Cozette Phifer, Cindy Ratzlaff, Jenny Robertson, Charly Rok, Danielle Romano, Kerri Ross, Elycia Rubin, Terry Savage, Diane Sawyer, Lee Schneller, Doborah Scott, Jill Scott, Roni Selig, Anne Sellaro, Rob Sheiffele, Adam Spiegelman, Lauren Synder, Katrina Szish, Joe Tacopino, Susan Taylor, Mark Turner, Christina Vandre, Claire Weinraub, and Scott Woodward.

Thanks to all out friends and family who have listened to us rant and rave nonstop about *Starring You!*—we appreciate your support, patience, and humor.

Thank you also to our friends at the New Venus Diner on Eighth Avenue in Chelsea, for allowing us to turn the second booth on the right into our office and writing workshop.

Finally, to all the great guest (and their ideas, products, or companies) who are about to become stars in the media or in their own lives. With all your potential, *Starring You!* serves its greatest purpose.

CONTENTS

	Foreword by Paula Deen	xiii
Chapter 1	The Power of the Glowing Box	1
Chapter 2	In the *TV Guide* of Life, Who Are You—and Why?	29
Chapter 3	Know the Shows!	52
Chapter 4	Perfect Pitch	83
Chapter 5	The Welcome Guest	119
Chapter 6	Expand Your TV Presence	157
Chapter 7	Show You the Money	192
Chapter 8	A Host of Options	219
Conclusion	Wrap Party—Are You Ready to Be a Star?	250
	Resources	252

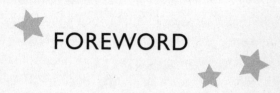

FOREWORD

Since you picked up this book, and are reading this little essay, I am going to share my most secret recipe with y'all:

Paula's Recipe for Success

Ingredients
1 part curiosity
1 part sincerity
1 part dedication
1 part hard work
2 parts interest in other people
2 parts passion

Instructions
Combine all six, and add a willingness to do whatever it takes to achieve your goal.

If you go after what you want using this recipe, the outcome will have moved you miles ahead of the other fellow. But let me also say that television was not part of my plan when I opened The Bag Lady in 1989, a lunch delivery service I started when

I was forty-two years old. Television was not in my thoughts back then. I was trying to use what I knew about cooking to support my two young sons and myself.

Through a series of events and being in the right place at the right time, and most of all, making good food that people liked and noticed (all of which you'll learn about in this book), a wonderful television producer with an interest in food named Gordon Elliot had me on his show, *Door Knock Dinners*. Now his company, Follow Productions, produces my Food Network shows—*Paula's Home Cooking* and *Paula's Party*—and even my sons' new show, *Road Tasted*. So television not only changed my life, it changed Jamie and Bobby's lives too. That is what makes television so magical—the way it can take regular people, bottle their passion, and transmit it to people all over the world. All of a sudden you have a million new friends.

It took many years of hard work to get where I am today and I wouldn't trade that time for anything. It was worth it. For those of you who dream about being a TV chef, a talk show host, or a guest expert, I want to say stay true to yourself, keep your feet on the ground, and always be honest with your audience. They know when you aren't 100 percent truthful. I think that's why women especially identify with me—I am an average woman in the home, and I never forget that. I conduct myself the same way now as I did when I was running all over Savannah delivering lunch to business people. I am grateful everyday for what I have.

I bring hope to people because they think, "If little ol' Paula can do it, anybody can"—and it's true. In *Starring You!* the authors make this point very clearly—no one gets very far for very long by being a phony. My advice to y'all who want to be on TV, but don't think it can ever happen, is first to know that it is possible. Look at me—I am not a professional chef or a trained journalist. But I did make a commitment to one thing, and I opened myself to the possibilities.

Develop your skill, and show your passion for it with a home video, a letter, or a Web site—and *read this book*. There is so much real-life, insider advice in *Starring You!* that only two experienced producers like Terence and Marta know. I especially love their advice to stick to what you know, and never take no for an answer. Keep trying. Be creative! Oh, and always have a little bit of funny.

I wish you love and best dishes—from my TV kitchen to yours.

Paula Deen

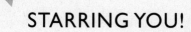

STARRING YOU!

Chapter 1

The Power of the Glowing Box

There are literally hundreds of shows, from local TV to *The Oprah Winfrey Show*, that depend on guests. The producers of these shows are constantly seeking new angles on stories, novel ideas, unique information, and fresh faces to deliver it all. For you, this translates into countless opportunities to get your message in front of millions of interested people. The most important thing to remember is this:

> There are more segments to fill
> than there are good people to fill them.

This is exactly why you often see the same guests and experts. Good people really *are* hard to find, and we are out to change that with this book. We think there are thousands of people who have untapped potential to use television effectively to enhance their businesses, to get particular messages out about causes, or even just to expand the horizons of their lives and at the same time entertain and inform viewers. That's really why we wrote this book—we *know* television changes lives and businesses. Just look at us—two regular kids from New Jersey and Long Island who followed our dreams to success in television!

Television transforms lives: it has the power to turn a small-town girl into an internationally known singing sensation (Kelly Clarkson), change a local business into a world-class operation (Shabby Chic), make a struggling author into an "overnight" sensation (Candace Bushnell), and catapult a charming morning talk show guest to the heights of hosting her own show (Suze Orman). Its hurricane-like force when it comes to promoting people, ideas, products, and services to large groups is unquestionable. With a bit of effort you can access TV's power—and that's what this book is all about.

For all the technology available today (streaming video, podcasts, cell phone applications, and so on) and pundits' predictions about the future of media and communication (all books will be stored on a tiny computer you carry in your pocket or even attached to your heads with wires. Hmmm . . .), we believe people will continue to gather information in traditional ways, while adapting to new forms of technologies as they develop. For now, the majority of us continue to get a great deal of entertainment and information from television. As we write this book, there are new media being developed that need content and talent, and which you can also exploit. But this book focuses on the power of TV because right now it's the most effective mass media tool there is.

Just look at the number of networks that have sprung up in the past twenty years. There used to be three major networks (CBS, NBC, and ABC), public TV (PBS), and a few small stations that showed cartoons and old movies, generally with snowy reception included for free. Starting in the late 1980s, the big three started feeling their first real competition: FOX launched in 1986; UPN and the WB were both launched independently in 1995 but subsequently merged to form CW in the fall of 2006; and PAX network began in 1998, but changed its name to I: Independent Television in 2005. Today there are also hundreds of local stations (most owned by one of these networks) and cable or "pay TV" networks, some devoting themselves to single topics, such as movies, fitness, entertainment, lifestyle, food, politics, or any number of other specific issues or interests targeted at particular audiences.

Much of the programming on these networks is informational or service- or reality-based, meaning the shows use guests to discuss topics, share ideas, and provide a service. There will always be movies, comedies, and dramas on television, particularly in prime time (8 P.M. to 11 P.M.), but the majority of television depends on non-actors discussing topics and ideas. New cable stations pop up all the time, and they can't book guests and experts fast enough. No matter what the technological vehicle, it is all about the search for new and better content—and people who can deliver it.

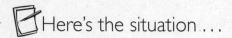 Here's the situation ....

There are a few terms you need to know right away, and they are:

Pitch: A concisely written (occasionally verbal) presentation of an idea for a television segment, which is sent to a show's producer or booker by e-mail or hand delivery. Verbal TV segment pitches can sometimes be made on the phone; they are rarely done in person.

Segment: Generally four to seven minutes of a news, talk, variety, or lifestyle show that deals with a single topic or issue. One-hour shows usually have seven seven-minute segments; half-hour shows can have four four-and-a-half-to-five-minute segments, but those times can vary.

Produce: In the simplest terms, when we "produce" a person or segment, it means we develop a segment concept around them, including pre-interviewing to establish talking points, writing scripts, making sure any visuals or props are in place, and preparing the host for the segment.

Terence

In the age of TiVo and Internet downloads, it's very simple for people to banish traditional commercials from their lives. Ads in magazines and newspapers are not as effective as they used to be. Getting time on a show, especially one that is specifically targeted to a sympathetic audience, is one of the most effective ways of getting your brand or idea or service in front of people who want to know about it. Such segments often represent a "third-party endorsement," which means that someone is either talking directly to you or saying something positive about you, your product, or idea because they believe in it, not because they are being paid to do so. "That kind of endorsement can make or break a company. That's a flip from five years ago, when advertising was the focus of brand development," says Jon Harris, vice president of media development and communications for the Fortune 50 Sara Lee Corporation.

The strategies in the book have universal application—learning to define yourself as a brand, clarify your message, and convince someone that your idea is worth paying attention to (or, eventually, paying for) in a crisp concise way are valuable tools whether you want to get on television, become head of your PTA, or land that dream job. It doesn't even matter if you never pitch yourself to a television producer—you'll get practical information here that you can use to make your everyday life better. Just the other day Terence rented a car and "produced" the woman at the rental agency, using the same techniques in this book, and got himself upgraded from an economy car to a luxury sports model.

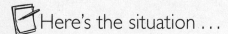Here's the situation ...

There are some surprising facts about getting booked on TV:

- Producers are constantly looking for new faces and ideas and will pay attention when interesting things cross their desks.

- Getting booked is not about looks or glamour—it's about being a great talker and delivering the goods.

- You do not have to have television experience or a special media or communications degree to get booked on a show.

- It is much easier to contact the right person at a TV show than you think. Just call the show and ask for the person who deals with your topic. Sometimes it can be that simple!

- Fancy press kits and elaborate tapes can be a waste of money: just tell a producer what's on your mind concisely and clearly.

Terence

We have brought together the top broadcasters, on-air talent, and people whose lives have been changed because of TV and we promised all of them that you were going to read this book. Their time is valuable and the fact that they have given some of it to us *and* revealed their secrets, pet peeves, and enthusiasm for the business is a *miracle*. It may be your only chance to hear from many of these people, including Diane Sawyer, Nancy Grace, Paula Deen, and Isaac Mizrahi, and producers at top shows, such as *Entertainment Tonight, Good Morning America,* and *The View.* Even if they have moved on to other jobs by the time you read this book, the advice they offer is still relevant and useful. You cannot put a dollar amount on this information—professional advice is expensive and hard to get . . . until now. Most of them have never been interviewed or written about. So don't show up on Nancy Grace's show or to cook with Paula Deen without having read *Starring You!* first.

Television people work hard—we've logged hundreds of hours in a week putting together a show and in Marta's case an entire network (she was one of the original development executives of E! Entertainment Television and the Style Network). When you get up in the morning bleary-eyed, struggling to get ready for the day, and you turn on the tube to get a morning dose of news, take a minute to think about the fact that the people on the screen have gotten up three or sometimes four hours before they appear on the air—and so have all the people behind the scenes who you never see. When watching the local part of the morning news shows, realize that the reporter covering the fire or the teacher's strike most likely got the assignment just hours before, reported on the story, wrote it, produced the segment herself, and then appeared on air telling you the story, looking pretty good on camera. Sometimes reporters even operate the camera themselves!

If you think you can do better than what's out there, maybe you can, but remember that what you see on television is the very best of what's available. In that sense the cream really does float to the top. If there were a formula, every show would be a hit. So much is done by instinct and gut feelings. Again, that means producers are willing to take chances. That's good for you.

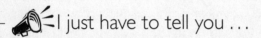

I just have to tell you …

There are three simple secrets to achieving your "starring role" on TV:

1. Have an idea you feel passionate about.
2. Do your research: know your shows, their content, and the talent in front of the camera, and the players behind the scenes.
3. Respect the time of the television pros you contact.

Marta

Here's the thing: this book is not about your "fifteen minutes of fame." It is about using television as part of a strategy to build a brand, broaden a business, or enhance your life. Television is a way of bringing your message to more people than you could meet in a lifetime, but it takes work on your part. We hope to demystify the process for you and offer strategies for getting booked and then conveying yourself and your message effectively, and over the long term.

Television presents an unmatched opportunity for personal and professional growth. Just look at some of these extraordinary success stories:

• In 1989 a talented interior designer introduced a new style of decorating that combined vintage design with a modern sensibility in her Santa Monica store. Comfort, the beauty of imperfection, the allure of time-worn objects, and the appeal of simple practical living are the cornerstones of what has become known as Shabby Chic. A successful line of books followed. The books and her shop came to the attention of a television executive . . . and soon Rachel Ashwell was hosting her own show based on her lifestyle philosophy. On her TV show and in her books, she was generous with her ideas and readily gave away the secrets to her style. Fourteen years, six specialty stores, a wholesale division, product licensing, four books, and fifty-six Style Network episodes later Rachel Ashwell's Shabby Chic brand remains as fresh and relevant as ever. The nationwide audience she garnered via TV exposure brought her to the attention of Target executives, who asked her to develop a Shabby Chic line for the mega-retailer. She's also developing a new TV show and opening up numerous new stores.

• A young woman struggling with her weight appeared on *The Rosie O'Donnell Show* to talk about an Ironman Triathalon she was training to compete in. Rosie was so inspired by her story she made her the leader of her Chub Club, an ongoing weight loss program sponsored by the show. The woman branded an entire program based on the appearance she made on Rosie. "It magnified what I was doing on a small level, and gave me a voice to share with thousands of people. It set the platform for what I do today," says Judy Molnar. Judy is now a nationally known certified personal trainer, fitness coach, motivational speaker, and author of a popular book based on her fitness and lifestyle program.

- An audition tape finds its way into the hands of an HBO producer. She loves the personality and energy of the young man on the tape and fights for him to be designated host of entertainment news segments. Flash forward several years and you can see that same man hosting the country's top-rated morning news show. Matt Lauer is one of the most popular hosts in the *Today* show's history.

- One day a television executive goes shopping in Los Angeles and comes across a home furnishing store called Maison Luxe. She loves the store and its owner's great style. The executive brings him to the Style Network to be one of the hosts of *Area*, an upscale home-design show. Producers from the network television program *Extreme Makeover: Home Edition* spot Michael Moloney and bring him on to be one of the hosts of that show. Michael is now a nationally recognized authority on home design as well as a television personality in his own right. He also has a new adult home-design line for Disney.

- A New York manicurist, known for her work with celebrities such as Mariah Carey, Sarah Jessica Parker, and George Clooney, started a small manicure product business nearly seven years ago in the living room of her tiny city apartment. TV gave her the chance to start that business—she would have no visibility without it. From an ongoing spot on *The Rosie O'Donnell Show* to a makeover on *The View*, Debbie Lippmann truly connects with her customers. "For a small brand like lippmann collection, TV exposure has given us an invaluable method of reaching out to a broad, national audience," she says.

- A producer sees potential in a young woman from a *Sur-*

vivor cast. She taps her to become the host of a cable fashion makeover show, *The Look for Less.* . . . It doesn't take long for the networks to notice and now Elisabeth Hasselbeck is a member of the hit daytime talk show *The View.*

Pretty amazing stories, aren't they? We know they are because each of us had a hand in all of these success stories . . . and we're proud to be able to say that. Let's take a closer look at one TV phenomenon that everyone is curious about.

The Big O

Most people know that an appearance on Oprah Winfrey's long-running talk show can be a life-altering experience. In fact, now whenever there is a dramatic aftereffect of an appearance on any TV show it's called the Oprah Effect, because Oprah has really been a force when it comes to rethinking how TV can be used to disseminate information to large numbers of people and influence their behavior (by getting them to buy a book or product, stop eating beef, or start a fitness routine).

Oprah is the ultimate third-party endorsement because viewers trust her so much. "Oprah handpicks her favorite things," concurs Amy Metrick Hornstein, executive director of Origins Natural Resources global communications. "In 2002, Oprah declared Origins's Perfect World body cream one of her favorite things, and for the following two months sales increased by 1,900 percent and it continues to sell strongly to this day," says Amy. It's a great product, but there is no way Origins could have let as many people know that without that kind of incredible backing.

A company doesn't snap its fingers and get support like that. Part of it is the luck of the draw, of course. "There is no correlation with what we have sent her and what she ends up using," says Amy. "We do not know if it is something she liked before we sent it or something she discovered, since the show never confirms anything," she explains. In the case of A Perfect World, Amy says Origins got a call from the show's producers asking if they could have a container for everyone in the audience. "We sent it," says Amy. Wise decision!

Oprah is also known for her support of books. For an author, getting on *Oprah* can be a mind-blowing experience to say the least. Just ask A. Manette Ansay.

"When I found out I was chosen by Oprah I had no idea what would happen," she says about her novel, *Vinegar Hill,* being selected for the TV host's book club in November 1999. "It brought me into a huge number of homes, and they trusted her. People still buy *Vinegar Hill*, it's in print and sold in bookstores. When I am on tour for a new book, it's always sold alongside the new book. As a literary writer I would not have expected that. It is amazing," she says.

The power of Oprah resonated further about a week after Manette was on the show and traveling in Anchorage, Alaska. "I went into a convenience store and the clerk looked at me and said, 'I know you, you were on *The Oprah Winfry Show.*' This happened for a week; every day I went out. TV's immediacy and ability to connect viewers amazes me."

All that said, you certainly do not have to get on *Oprah* to reap the benefits of television appearances. Countless people have had success without ever appearing on that show. We think that is an important point: so many people we meet say to us, "We want the *Today* show, we want *Oprah,*" and that may not be possible, or even necessary to promote your ideas. Many of the people in this book have never been on either show (and some who have been on both).

Spotlight On: Michael Moloney

In 1993, after ten years in the fashion industry, Michael Moloney turned his design concepts to home furnishings. Blending the new and the practical with the charm of things "not exactly perfect." has been Michael's look from the beginning of his interior design career, when he opened Le Garage in Redondo Beach, California. His style combines vintage treasures, new accessories, and giftware. His eclectic, fresh approach to decorating took off and, a few years later, Michael opened Maison Luxe in Manhattan Beach, California, stocking it with all things luxurious from France and Italy, which he handpicks. Michael's television credits include guest appearances on *The Christopher Lowell Show, Next Door with Katie Brown, Kitty Bartholomew: You're Home, Designers' Challenge, Area, Clean House,* and *Extreme Makeover: Home Edition.*

Starring You!: *How did your first appearance on TV occur?*
Michael Moloney: My very first one was on *The Christopher Lowell Show.* I had always traveled overseas to buy antiques. That's what my stores are known for. One of Christopher's producers knew my work, and I was asked to do a segment on French flea markets. Then Kitty Bartholomew and Katie Brown happened, and that's when Marta [Tracy] came into the picture. She and her colleague at E! Network were customers in my shop and they said you need to be on TV and I said okay bring it on! So they put me on the Style Network design show *Area.* It was a fun, hip makeover show. Then came *Clean House.* I have always had the entertainment bug

and I am gregarious and had modeled and acted, so it was natural. *But I tell you—the very best part you can play is yourself.* It is easier and more convincing. When you are offering information and advice, people have to believe you. It lets me forget about the camera.

SY: *Did your business change when you became a regular on the Style Network?*
MM: TV solidified my credibility. It is validating for people, they think, This guy knows his stuff, and that speaks volumes when someone hires a designer. I have gotten more high-end design work through TV.

SY: *So you are still actively involved in the stores?*
MM: That's my core and I will never lose it. You have to stay true to yourself and your brand. If you have a store, that's what you are. TV wants you for what you do and who you are. Don't try to put on airs, just be who you are, and success will follow.

SY: *Has your design sensibility evolved as your media experiences have broadened?*
MM: My taste has certainly changed. It's now more contemporary, elegant, whimsical, and eclectic. In fact, that's why Disney was interested in me—I recently inked a deal with them to design home furnishings for adults.

SY: *What's next?*
MM: I will stay with *Extreme Makeover: Home Edition* for as long as I can. Right now I am realizing my anonymity is no longer mine—I just got back from Greece

and they recognized me there! It's been great but it's one thing to do a cable show and quite another to do a national network show. It is a whole other level, and thank God people like it! I want to do more hosting and red carpet coverage for TV Guide's channel and the Emmys and Golden Globe Awards. I am not really sure I want my own show. I enjoy hosting. It's really important to take every opportunity and use it as a chance to fine-tune your craft. I did *The View* recently, which is live. I would not have been able to do well on a live format show a few years ago.

Maybe you just want to have some fun and expand the borders of your life. That's what happened to New Jersey housewife Brenda Murphy when she reached out for tickets but instead got a call from Terence, who was then a producer at *The Rosie O'Donnell Show*. It changed her life very unexpectedly and in truly remarkable ways. Brenda didn't even want to be a guest on television; she wasn't selling anything or trying to become famous. All she wanted was a chance to sit in the audience of the popular show. Brenda wrote to Rosie because she loved her program, not because she had any intention of building a business or becoming a media star.

We sat down with Brenda to find out exactly what she sent Rosie and what happened to her as a result.

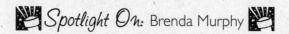 Spotlight On: Brenda Murphy

The Candy Queen

Starring You!: *Brenda, you've been making special cakes and candy creations for your daughters and neighborhood kids for years. What was it that inspired you to create something special for* The Rosie O'Donnell Show?

Brenda Murphy: I wrote for tickets to Rosie and just could never get any. I thought if I made a replica of her studio out of candy and sent them pictures of it, maybe they would give me a couple of tickets.

SY: *That's an understatement compared to what actually happened. You made something pretty elaborate and accurate.*

BM: Well, I taped the show and studied her studio very carefully, including how her desk was situated and where the camera people stood. I constructed the set with candy—including painting guests' faces on M&Ms. I took pictures and sent them in, along with a friendly note asking for tickets to the show. The next thing I knew I got a call—Rosie wanted me as a *guest*!

SY: *You seem to have intuitively known how to pitch a producer—send something authentic and personal and eye-catching, accompanied by a concise but enthusiastic note. What was the appearance like?*

BM: I was on cloud nine! Rosie and I hit it off and she really liked the candy set—Rosie loves crafts so it really caught her eye. Then I went home and I thought that was it—my little dream had come true.

SY: *But you didn't just rest on your laurels after that!*

BM: Shortly after the appearance, I entered a Nabisco contest and built a house with thirty of their products, and was selected as a finalist. Since I had sold cakes in the past, I entered the contest as an adult professional. The night before the big show, we had dinner with our competition. Oh boy! One person had a degree from Harvard, another a badge from Yale, yet I won and went right back on *Rosie* with my winning project! It was featured in *Good Housekeeping* and on the now-defunct *Later Today*. I made many other appearances on Rosie's show after that. When the show was finally going to end in 2002, I created a special cake for the final episode. It was a spectacular six-tiered farewell cake, which featured edible pictures of the guests from each of the show's six seasons. Rosie was so overwhelmed by it that she spontaneously gave my husband and me a vacation in Hawaii!

SY: *So, basically, you became a regular on Rosie's show?*

BM: Yes, I really did! I still find it so amazing that I have been on numerous TV shows, including *The Tony Danza Show* and *The Wayne Brady Show,* all because of Terence and one of Rosie's other producers, Fran Brescia. And I never thought I would have a children's book written about me—*Candy Creations from the Candy Queen* (Mondo Publishing) is used in schools to encourage children to read biographies. I am also featured as "the Candy Queen" in several Winged Tiger and Patrick Rabbit comic books.

SY: *Talk about playing with your food! Give us an idea of what other things have happened to you since your first appearance on* Rosie *in 1998.*

BM: Oh my, there have been so many opportunities. I created a candy replica of Times Square with a candy ball dropped, changing from 1999 to 2000 and that was used during the televised celebration. I was at the New York Chocolate Show in 2001 as a special guest. Recently my candy dinosaurs were on display at the Cleveland Museum of Natural History. I took part in Laura Bush's National Book Festival in Washington, D.C., and I have created special gift bags for Dena Hammerstein's Only Make Believe, a New York City charity for terminally ill children. I made a candy replica of the stage and actors for the opening of Kathie Lee Gifford's musical *Under the Bridge* and a candy replica of the Plymouth Theatre and candy favors for Rosie's show *Taboo*.

SY: *You've also demonstrated your techniques at the ICES convention in Las Vegas and made visits to the Food Network,* The Caroline Rhea Show *…*

BM (Laughs): Yes, and I have done candy work for Disney (that was an edible abstract mosaic of Mickey Mouse, made of M&Ms!) and the International Tennis Hall of Fame—and so many other wonderful things!

SY: *It sounds like your life has really changed. What's the secret for getting booked on these shows?*

BM: Yes, I had a very happy life before I went on *Rosie*, but these opportunities have added such fun and excitement. I think the secret is, do what you love and be willing to share it with others. **If you do get on TV, maintain relationships with producers you meet, because they go from show to show and they remember you.**

TV gets a bad rap sometimes, but we don't think it should. How can you not feel warm and fuzzy toward the tube when you meet somebody like Brenda? Not every guest has television potential, nor is every show a winner (producers are people too—and can make mistakes) you may not like everything on television, but there is a lot that's good. Let's not take it for granted.

Our own paths to careers in television are very different— another reason we wanted to write *Starring You!* We are like a lot of people who work in broadcasting: We did not come from show business backgrounds or families; we were not really "connected" in any way. But here we are, developing and producing shows, scouting talent, and loving every minute of it. We have met so many amazing people, both guests and colleagues. That's another benefit TV has over other mediums. What other vehicle brings together such a diverse number of people? On a single show or network you see actors and actresses, professional journalists, scientists, stylists, politicians, chefs, musicians, and more. Working in segment and information TV is like going to a really fabulous New York cocktail party every night.

So, without further ado, we want you to know a little bit about who we are before you get deep into the book.

Marta's Story: Einstein and Me

Everyone needs a dream to pull them from one place to another. It's a passion that becomes a hunger. For me it was twofold. First, I grew up in New Jersey watching *That Girl,* and I wanted to work in a big city with a *really* exciting job. Second, I have always been interested in lifestyle and child-related topics. I was at Boston College, studying early childhood education with aspirations to teach. One of my internships put me in direct contact with special needs kids. The classroom situation was limited and confining, and I found myself getting too emotionally attached to the kids to be an effective teacher. I thought, This is not right for me; I need a much bigger box.

As luck would have it I was in the lower level of the education building, and I saw a sign on a door that read TV 101. Standing in front of that door, weighed down by textbooks, I had one of my first "Einstein Moments (EMs)": I could marry my interest in children with my interest in TV.

So I enrolled in as many of BC's communications classes as I could, and all my feelings from that initial EM were confirmed. The course work and an internship at WGBH TV gave me energy and passion for TV, and it could not be stopped—it was like grass growing through concrete. Before I had even really begun studying I had 100 percent clarity about wanting to work in TV. It seemed different and exciting: it was the big box I was looking for.

There was only one problem. I had graduated but had no contacts in media. No one in my immediate family knew anyone. My parents started asking everyone they knew if there was anyone even remotely connected to television they could introduce me to.

My uncle Bob was in the newspaper delivery and distribution business, and he knew someone who worked at CBS who in turn knew the producer of *Captain Kangaroo*. That's a pretty weak link, but it's how I got my first job in children's television—after three years of pounding the pavement. It took me that long to figure out that you call in May to get a job in September on a seasonal program. Talk about persistence! When you have the bug to do something, you have to chip away at it, and that includes asking everyone you know whom he or she knows and knocking on a lot of doors. We are all connected to one another. Someone you know knows somebody else and so on.

While it took me three years to get into children's TV, my first job out of college was at HBO, a new concept in television broadcasting: commercial free, uncut and unedited movies, sports, specials, and comedy. I helped developed HBO Entertainment News reports, and went to bat for an unknown, Matt Lauer, to host them. After that I helped launch a cable network called E! Entertainment Television, and later created its sister network, the Style Network.

It is now thirty years since I first started in the business. I have watched TV make and break careers—I have watched on-air host Greg Kinnear turn from a funny guy on E! Entertainment's *Talk Soup* to an extraordinary movie star and incredible actor. I have watched *PM Magazine* host Matt Lauer become the phenomenally popular head anchor on the *Today* show. I marvel at how Joan Rivers continually uses TV to reinvent herself. I have watched TV bring a new audience to Howard Stern and seen people no one has ever heard of find themselves the "loser" on a reality show to then being on *The View* with Barbara Walters—that's Elisabeth Hasselbeck. Rachel Ashwell grew her Shabby Chic idea from a store in California to a series of beautiful books to a show on the Style Network to a lucrative licensing deal with Target stores and more.

TV offers tremendous careers for women. The world of television production is very open to us; one recent report I read said that men are now the minority in the field, and I believe it. When I got my first job, I remember thinking that I wanted to make $30,000 by the time I was thirty. Well, I am happy to say I far surpassed that. I did not go into TV for the money, yet it turned out to be a very lucrative career. It has given me an amazing creative outlet and a chance to meet and network with the most fascinating people on earth.

Yes, it's true that there are treacherous people in TV, as there are in all businesses and in life. But I have navigated the waters and gravitated toward the highest-caliber companies and people I could find; those with the values and standards I share. It can also be a world of nos and meanness and disappointment— one day it is an industry that embraces you body, mind, and spirit, and the next day it can chew you up and spit you out. Perseverance, as a talent on camera and behind the scenes, as well as in life, is paramount to success in this business. I have faced adversity in my own life—I was at the top of my game, running the Style Network, and then my professional and personal lives changed dramatically. I had to leave a job I loved because of major management changes. Then my husband died suddenly and very tragically, and I had a teenage son I had to provide for. Writing this book has been one of my paths to healing. It reflects what I love to do best: working with and shepherding talent and creating content. Now I have my own media company, working with entrepreneurs and businesses to develop brands on TV and across multiple media platforms.

Everybody wants to be on TV—or at least it seems that way to me. Terence and I outline proven ways to get there, which we have collected through personal experience in cable and syndication. The truth is there is no single way to get on TV. It is a process of trial and error, persistence, doing many things and repeating what works, and reinventing yourself along the way to fit the needs of the producers of different shows throughout the country and the world. Trial and error and the insider information in this book give you your best shot.

Terence: **X Marks the Spot**

After almost fifteen years of working in television, I still re-member my first day as a CBS page as if it were yesterday. In fact, I still have my uniform. The network used to send me letters requesting that I send it back but I never did because I want my kids to wear it on Halloween! They have finally given up all hope of having it returned.

Each day I went to the Ed Sullivan Theater to work at the *Late Show with David Letterman* and saw the many people who lined up for a chance to be in the audience. There was a bar next to the theater and the other pages and I would go there after the show was over and people would treat us like celebrities! They wanted to buy us drinks and take pictures with us, and, of course, it was fantastic for us because we had no money and were just starting out. After I took part in one Letterman skit people noticed me on the street. Right then I knew how powerful TV was.

Growing up, TV was a safe place. I wasn't good at sports, I felt different from everyone in school, and I always connected with what was going on in the world that I saw on TV—from the news to game shows to drama and comedy. In fact, I always wanted to be a contestant on *The Price Is Right*. I was devastated when I learned that competitors weren't just picked randomly from the audience. My friend Melissa went to the show, and later told me that the producers made everyone line up beforehand and they prepicked the people whose names would later be called "by surprise."

When I was sixteen my friend Aly Elish and I tried out for *Club MTV*. At the time it was their version of *American Bandstand*. We cut school and road the Long Island Rail Road into the city. For the audition, they made us dance on a big X on the floor. There were a lot of people lined up, but I still remember this one guy who was so desperate to be on the show. The casting people said he looked too old because he had a beard so he actually left, had it shaved, came back, and tried to audition again. I do not want to brag, but we did make it to the semifinals. We did not make it to the finals (they had the nerve to tell me I was too preppy!) but I just loved trying out.

In college I wanted to be an agent: I got accepted into the mailroom program at one of the top agencies, but I did not end up there. I knew instinctively it was not for me because I am so interested in other people's stories and finding out what makes them tick. Once I started producing I realized it was the perfect fit. My first television job, if you could call it that, was as an assistant in television corporate sales. I had set my sights on becoming a producer, so every day after work I would drop my résumé off with the security guard at CBS. I asked everyone I knew if they knew someone at the network I could talk to. I did not give up. That was my first *Starring You!* experience. Since then, I've won four daytime Emmy Awards and have been privileged to work with Rosie O'Donnell, Ellen De-

Generes, Montel Williams, Katie Brown, and Isaac Mizrahi, as well as for CBS News and *The Early Show,* NBC, TBS, Sony, and now at FOX.

As I fast-forward I am still in awe of TV; I am not jaded about it in the least because I know what one appearance can do for you (if done right). Going from unknown to regularly featured expert to hosting a show is not impossible. Even some appearances on local television can make a small business. When I read about how the Internet, webcasts, and podcasts are changing media, I think, Yes, that's all well and good but all that technology still stems from and is influenced by television. There is nothing more powerful than sharing your message via TV.

I remember at the Golden Globes one year, E! Entertainment Television was doing a preshow special on the red carpet and the actress Keira Knightley held up the lipstick she was using, and within twenty-four hours that lipstick was sold out at every Sephora in the country. People want to be associated with celebrity, with what's fabulous, and with what they think other people are talking about. Where else can you get a message about your brand to people on such a level other than on television?

One time, I needed a T-shirt with a particular message printed on it for my friend Jeff's birthday. And I needed it fast. So I called a fairly large New York clothing manufacturer and explained my dilemma to the owner. He said no way could it be done. Then I mentioned that I worked for a major television studio and before I even finished my sentence, his tune changed. He stopped production as soon as we hung up, made that T-shirt, and had it for me by the end of the day. It hit me again: TV is power. I mean, if you can stop an entire clothing factory to make one T-shirt, well, that's something, isn't it?

It is a simple concept if you think about it—you create a good idea or a brand and put yourself in the media and let the world come to you. On the other hand, I am still shocked to this day at how ill prepared professional and intelligent people are when it comes to using the power of TV. I know there are some people who do not watch TV, but even if you are in a luxury business and think you are above it all, you're not. It kills me to see how many people miss opportunities that could change their lives and their careers for the better.

Many people think they have no chance, that there is no way they are going to get a call back and get a booking. Wrong! We are all looking for a great new idea or the best new guests, products, and brands. That's what we are doing—and we all want to be the first to have it on the show and to break the star, the idea, the personality. We meet people all the time in our regular lives who we say should be on TV and they turn around and say they have no idea who to call . . . or what to do . . .

Marta and I recently worked on a mini pilot (a short version of a potential television show) and tested four people as on-air talent. We sent everyone the material four or five days in advance, and on the day of the shoot one of the people was simply not prepared. It was as if she had never even opened the envelope we had sent. I am done with that person. Producers are smart enough to know the signs that say stay away. They see trouble on the horizon and they are not going to go there—they will not bring in people who are going to make it worse. They are busy enough.

Preparation is just one of the things both of us advocate. Yes, it is possible to be on television, but it does require effort and if you are not willing to make the effort, well, then it's probably not for you. But if you want to put in some time and thought—oh, the places you can go!

How to Use This Book

Starring You! lays out a clear step-by-step strategy to get your personality, special knowledge, idea, product, or company on television (or simply noticed by the right non-TV people) and parlay it into a career and recognition on or off the screen. We share many real-life stories and authentic examples of how TV works and changes lives. It's based on our combined experience (more that forty years' worth) spent on the front lines and in the trenches of producing TV, helping mold people's on-air careers. The book is based on the model we use when clients come to us to learn the skills they need to get booked on television and make their TV appearances a success. In essence, we teach people how to become TV stars.

We want this to be not only an informational reading experience but also a fun one! And while we are writing in unison as one voice, there are certain times when we each "take you aside" and give you some of our own favorite individual advice ("I just have to tell you . . ." is Marta's favorite expression, and "Here's the situation . . ." is Terence's).

"Spotlight On" features are Q&A interviews with people we think you'll be excited about hearing from one-on-one— especially since most if not all of them have never been interviewed about what they do and how they do it. And there are even a few round-table discussions—where several people in one sector of the industry weigh in on a topic. Occasional round tables gather experts from one area together to drill deeply into certain aspects of the business, such as local TV or working behind the scenes. The benefit of that is you get a glimpse into their worlds from the inside, which you are not going to find anyplace else.

The book progresses from finding your TV persona to understanding which shows use guests to pitching to developing TV relationships to maybe—just maybe—getting your own regular TV gig or hosting job. If you don't end up on your own personal sound stage, at least you'll understand how it can happen. We think it's a good idea to read through the book without jumping ahead. **We've written the book in this order for a reason: a potentially great pitch, made without the proper preparation, could be wasted.**

The best part about the strategies presented here is that you can use them to become the star of your own life, even if you don't want to be on the tube. Relationship building and learning how to get a message across succinctly are useful in just about every situation we can think of.

Finally, after you do our useful assignments (which are placed throughout the book) and put our suggestions into practice you will be ready to pitch your brand or to get that great job. By the way, we would love to hear your *Starring You!* success stories—please write and tell us about them online at www.starring-you.com.

 It's a Wrap

- There are more segments to fill than there are good people to fill them.
- Define what you want to accomplish.
- Develop effective pitches and presentations.

- Target pitches to the right TV shows.

- Follow up with producers and bookers.

- Prepare yourself to be a dream guest.

- Parlay one appearance into additional television segments or become a regular.

- Keep in touch and develop relationships with producers and behind the scenes VIP players.

- Handle the aftermath of your successful appearance graciously, and build on it.

- Increase your chances of obtaining lucrative licensing, media, and publishing deals.

- Look to the future new media and plan your place in it.

Chapter 2

In the *TV Guide* of Life, Who Are You—and Why?

The first brick you need to build your house of TV stardom (before studying the shows you want to get booked on or trying to craft a pitch) is a definition of who you are and what your message is. In other words, you need a platform. This word is bandied about everywhere from publishing to Hollywood. What is a platform? In our business it refers to a person's set of beliefs and expertise, usually supported by a unique backstory or particular life or professional circumstances, which brought him to his position and which allows the person to grasp the attention of some sector of the public. Whew. Lack of one is often used as an excuse not to book someone on a show: "She's got nothing to say." Or "His platform isn't strong enough," meaning he has a platform, but we just don't think it's very interesting. That, friend, is where the subjective nature of this business comes in. One man's authentic and persuasive platform is another man's hackneyed press release.

It's surprising how many people we meet say they want to be on television but have not really thought about what it is they have to offer in terms of their expertise, personality, and knowledge. Yet you are president of You, Inc., and in that role you have a responsibility to come to the table with a strong point of view and passion, otherwise there will be little reason for a producer to take a chance on you. It's not enough to want to be on television for the sake of it. If that's all you want, close the book now, go to New York City, and stand outside one of the morning shows—and wave. You need a good reason for appearing on television: your platform. And it all starts with your passion and persona and asking yourself how the audience will benefit by listening to you.

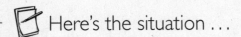 Here's the situation …

Stay true to yourself

Don't feel you have to imitate established personalities or brands. Always stay true to yourself and work on refining what makes you different and unique. **Producers don't want copies; they want originals.** You'll meet many people in this book who attribute their success to being themselves. Look at Food Network star Paula Deen—she was making down home food when nouvelle cuisine was in vogue. She also had none of the attributes that are supposedly "mandatory" in a TV personality: she was not young, model-gorgeous (although she's beautiful), or rail thin. She is, however, charming, a very good cook, and passionate about food and entertaining and people.

Terence

What's Your Story: Building a Platform

"Facts tell, stories sell," says Lash Fary, a product placement pro and an expert at pitching ideas to television. We love that quote because it says it all. Whether you are looking for one-off opportunities to teach Martha a recipe on her show, get your apartment shown on a design show, or be made over by a fashion stylist; have a more grand scheme to become a regular guest or expert on talk shows; want to promote a specific product; or even get your own show, there is a common denominator among people who have made TV work for them. They have another, defined purpose that is not about TV: an interesting backstory.

It is very similar to creating a character for a book or screenplay—only your "character" is real! A screenwriter or a novelist generally creates entire lives for their characters, even if the details never come up in the book or movie. The backstory informs that character's motivations and behavior and allows the writer to create a believable narrative. **Your backstory is what makes you relatable to the audience.**

Candy Queen Brenda Murphy always talks about how she was not looking for anything but to see Rosie and share her love for candy crafts. That very focused yet entirely sincere and guileless approach worked for Brenda. It was a happy surprise that her adorable backstory—creative candy lady makes replica of TV host's set because she wants tickets to her show—would have reverberations beyond simply sitting in the *Rosie* audience.

We love the story of the woman who sat down and wrote a letter to Oprah in which she described how she was redoing her house and ran out of money (anyone who has ever renovated her house knows this is an easy pickle to get in), and now she and her family were stuck without a kitchen. That is a story producers cannot make up—even if they thought, Let's find a person who has no kitchen, where would they look? Not only did Oprah's designer renovate the woman's kitchen, she actually redecorated her entire house, simply for the cost of a really great story.

If you want to build a brand or promote something you've produced, the Oprah story and Brenda Murphy's experience are relevant. A good platform starts with a compelling story. What is *your* story and what are you hoping to get out of sharing your passion with an audience?

It's very annoying to meet with someone who does not know what they are talking about or who does not seem to come by his or her supposed interest and knowledge organically. His story doesn't seem to be a real part of who he is; it does not come from his core or his heart. We talk a lot about what is authentic. We know it sounds a little "out there," but you have experienced what we mean. You can smell a phony a mile away. So can producers. We know a couple producers who wanted to develop a lifestyle show for women. They met with a woman who professed to solve all sorts of household problems. Her platform was a problem-solving business, and her employees solved the problems. She was the "face" of the company. Her backstory involved being stranded at home in a blackout and having to figure out how to keep her family warm and fed.

From that a business of home survival tools and equipment was born. Great! The problem was that she really did not know how to do any of the things she claimed to be able to do. It would be difficult for her to sustain a how-to show, since she would not be able to come through on any level. The producers passed on using her. While she had a platform and a backstory, she could not deliver real-time information or demonstrations. The producers knew viewers at home would instantly recognize the so-called expert was nothing of the sort. The problem solver would have been better off selling herself in another way—perhaps as a person who sought out the very best problem solvers and showcased their talents (unfortunately her ego would not allow her to do that).

☆ Advocate First: Nancy Grace

When CNN and Court TV journalist and host Nancy Grace got the call to be the legal expert on a struggling cable news network called News Talk TV many years ago, she was not thinking, This is my ticket to becoming a television personality. Far from it. But little did she know that it was Terence on the other end of that phone. She was passionate about victims' rights and the law, and she saw television as an opportunity to get her message across. She would tape TV segments in Atlanta at nine at night, after a long day at work as a special prosecutor in the Fulton County District Attorney's Office working on felony cases involving serial murder, rape, child molestation, and arson. Her work for the DA brought her to the attention of local and, eventually, national print and broadcast media.

"I never watched TV except for *Murder, She Wrote,* so all I knew was that this show wanted me to discuss current-day crime and victims' rights and, frankly, being a crime victim, I felt that here was a chance for me to speak out on behalf of crime victims," she recalls of those early days. "I'd go to a room on the eleventh floor, and there was a speakerphone and I would talk into it and I would have no idea of who it was or what it was. A voice would come on and start asking me questions, and I would just tear into the topic with everything I had. I was never even sure if anyone was listening or watching! But it was a chance to get my views across, and that was paramount to me."

Nancy's story is at turns both heartbreaking and inspiring. She gave up her plan to become an English professor after the murder of her fiancé. That led her to enroll in law school and become a prosecutor and victims' rights advocate. The combination of a seminal, tragic experience, her unerring support of crime victims, and her role as a dynamic and effective courtroom lawyer made her an extremely compelling expert *with a platform*—and she was smart enough to know that television is a format that reaches people she would never get to communicate with otherwise.

"Passion is not something you learn in law or journalism school. I really believe you have to stand for something with all your heart. It doesn't matter if you are on a speakerphone in an anonymous hotel room, sitting in a fancy television studio addressing millions of people per minute, or standing in front of twelve people in a jury box. My point of view comes across and the detractors cannot chip away at it. My goal then and now is to fight for victims' rights. Everything stems from that," Nancy says. That central theme runs through everything she does and has become her defining characteristic, or platform, in terms of TV.

Brand Me

Here's an assignment: Consider the following questions. Your answers help define yourself and your message and construct a platform. In fact, the answers to these questions now is helpful in going through all the stages of developing your career or mission on and off the small screen.

1. How did my interest, expertise, or product come about?
2. How have my past experiences brought me to this point?
3. What are my passions?
4. What are my strengths?
5. What skills do I need to develop or strengthen?
6. What are the ideal shows to guest on?
7. How do I want the appearance to specifically help achieve my goal?
8. What do I bring to the table that other people in my field do not bring?
9. Why do I want to be on TV?
10. Why do I think I would be good on TV?
11. What are ten things I can talk knowledgeably and confidently about?
12. If I were writing a book, what would the title be?
13. Most important, how will the audience benefit from what I have to offer?

Take a Letter! Krista Wrenn

Some people who do have the goods sell themselves short. We worked with Krista Wrenn, who designs very beautiful stationery for her own company, which is called Twenty-Seven. She was so busy creating these very high-end cards and writing paper that she forgot who she was. Krista did not realize that she had a lot more going for her than the very expensive notes and envelopes she designed. When we sat down and talked to her and asked her these ten questions (see box, "Brand ME"). It turned out she was from a small town in the South (a region of the country known for hospitality and gracious entertaining) and her interest in making beautiful stationery came out of the fact that her mom made all her birthday invitations when she was a child. That's what got her started. We also found out that she had created invitations and birth announcements for a few celebrity couples.

To producers like us Krista's background story is so much more compelling and relatable than the $35 custom-made invitations on their own. Gorgeous goods *and* a great story helped get her booked on shows. That combination allowed us to target the right programs and tailor pitches based on her personal narrative. For example, since Krista was now a hospitality expert from the South she could talk about the best ways to invite people to a dinner party during holiday entertaining segments on the morning shows. Whenever celebrities were expecting babies she could go on the entertainment segment of a news show and discuss the hippest ways celebs were announcing the birth of their babies—she was now an expert in these matters.

Once you have defined yourself, you have to be willing to

open your area of expertise without getting away from your core. If you are a lawyer there are many topics you can talk about—what are they? Look at Nancy Grace again. She is a prosecutor by trade and a victims' rights advocate. Yet she has always been willing to discuss all sorts of legal issues and does so with authority because she knows herself well and has honed her skills. "I would study up on and research any legal issue I was asked about because I was always thinking, This is a chance for me to speak out and become known for what I believe in. When someone gives you a chance, you go with it," she advises. It's important to see that she is not trying to be a lifestyle expert or a political pundit. She stays within her realm but is willing to expand it within her topic. Can you do that with your area? How broad can you make it without losing sight of your core message and persona?

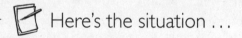 Here's the situation …

Don't give up your day job …

When you start getting booked on shows, it does not mean it is your new gig. Remember what got you on TV to begin with and stick with it. It's what will keep you on TV. I have seen many people crash and burn because they gave up what they were about, thinking they could replace it with a television career. It's not that simple.

Terence

Smile Style: Dr. Marc Lowenberg

Dr. Lowenberg is a New York dentist whose work and expertise, along with that of his partner, Dr. Gregg Lituchy, is regularly featured on several national television programs, including *Oprah, Good Morning America, Today, The View, CBS Evening News, Extreme Makeover,* and *Live with Regis and Kelly.* This exposure has really helped his business, making him one of the most sought-after, successful dentists in the country, with his own show and a line of products in development. Now, Dr. Lowenberg is a very good dentist—and he is not planning to leave dentistry anytime soon. Yet he recognizes that he is not the only great dentist in America. So why does he get so many prestigious bookings?

"I will tell you this for sure," he says. "Part of our success is that not only do you have to be very good at what you do, but you have to convey an appealing personality. The feedback I get from both producers and people who come to me seeking dentistry is that I am very approachable and real. I try hard to exude warmth and sensitivity, whether I am with a patient or on a TV set." Dr. Lowenberg is definitely the Marcus Welby type in person.

The dentist doesn't try to hide that aspect of his personality just because he is on TV. On the contrary, hiding behind some other "television persona" would be a mistake. "I get so many e-mails that say, 'I have been afraid of dentists all of my life, but I saw you on television and you seem so caring and friendly, I want to come and see you,'" he says. Dr. Lowenberg also has mind-blowing "before" and "after" visuals, and in TV that counts. "The photos are great, they are dramatic, but it's really presentation and character that put you over with viewers," he said. We could not agree more. The platform "dentist" is not enough. The persona "friendly dentist who can make a dramatic difference in your life" (with visuals and clients to prove it) is.

Food for Thought: Deborah Scott

We think Deborah is a great example of a chef who has a definite persona and a strong local platform, which she uses to get booked on local television (more on the importance of local TV in chapter four) to spread the word about the unique eateries she oversees in San Diego, California. Her Kemo Sabe restaurant is in the Hillcrest section of town and features food prepared with unique blends of spices and chiles. Patrons also delight in the artistic way she plates the food—colorful and rustic, it has become part of her signature and her story. Indigo Grill, located in San Diego's Little Italy, offers an eclectic blend of native foods originating in places as far flung as Oaxaca, Mexico, and Alaska.

Initially Deborah wanted to find a way to get the word out to the local community about her restaurant, Kemo Sabe, and that's what prompted her to make a television appearance: "I think it had to be about twelve years ago, in conjunction with a chef of the year award and wanting to talk about my restaurant on the news and knowing that in general people are interested in hearing about local restaurants and chefs and that interest is a draw for local stations, who want to appeal to their viewers' curiosity."

There are certain elements that set Deborah's story apart. She comes from the South and a tradition of hospitality and food. "I talk to all the guests in the dining room and they love the southern accent," she says. It has the same effect on the viewers when she is on TV. She also creates very classic cuisine injected with some culinary surprises. "For example, I try to combine cuisines. One is Asian and Southwest fusion. Mixing ingredients that are not normally combined to create some-thing beautiful and delicious is very intriguing to my customers and to local shows looking for a unique food segment." The use of disparate flavors to create delicious dishes is as impor-tant to Deborah's culinary style as it is to her media platform.

 I have to tell you ...

When it comes to TV, people fall into three buckets:

1. Those experts who undeniably have the personality and confidence to be successful as a guest or a host on TV with very little work. They're "naturals."

2. Those who need practice conveying their message and media coaching but have media potential.

3. Those who simply do not have what it takes for small-screen success. They should hire someone else to be their spokesperson, and work behind the scenes themselves.

Marta

"The other thing to remember is that when you are dem-onstrating a recipe on television, much of the preparation is done off camera, before the segment begins [you'll learn more about food prep and stylists in chapter six]. It is not a matter of demonstrating how to cook something—it is much more about your personality," says Deborah. She's right: more than any-thing people want to be entertained. She takes care of all the tedious prep work beforehand so she can wow viewers with her visuals—the completed dish—and her personality. "They want to look at the food in stages, they do not want to watch you chop onions. And they really want to hear about your ex-periences with the food and how your life experiences relate to what you are cooking," she says. There's that personal narra-tive again! As a result of her self-knowledge and original style, Deborah is one of a handful of San Diego chefs who appears regularly on local television.

Make a Name for Yourself

Deborah's successful restaurants were her original calling card. **If you have a business, you have to think of it as your living pitch.** This is particularly true if you are in any kind of lifestyle-oriented business such as restaurants, fashion, or home design. Rachel Ashwell first made her name as a store owner, and that caught the attention of a book publisher and the media. Michael Moloney also started with a couple of fabulous home-design stores in California, which caught the eye and imagination of television executives at Style. Despite the fact that Michael is now a busy TV design expert, he still has his shops and re-mains true to that core interest, which is what makes him such an effective TV personality.

Deborah Scott has chosen, for the moment, to stay local. However, it would not be challenging for her to build a na-tional platform using local press attention as a springboard, via books (she's had little time to devote to such a project, but will likely get around to it sometime soon), a Web site, a newspaper column, articles in appropriate magazines, and national TV interviews, speaking engagements, and national television demos. All of these outlets and methods are effective ways of increasing and broadening your platform, whether you are a cook or not.

A clear, easy-to-navigate Web site also gives you credibility, especially if you make a product or offer a service. We think a Web site is essential if you are planning on branding yourself to the media. The best part of a Web site is that it gives producers and other media an easy way to learn about you and your message. It also gives you a reason to promote yourself when you are on TV—and you can use it to sell products or books and to share news about you or your business. Refer producers to your site when pitching via e-mail, make photographs and video clips available and downloadable on it, and constantly update it with fresh content and news.

A Web site does not have to be elaborate, and the personal aspects of your life should play only a small part in the site (and your pitches in general) as they directly relate to your message and persona. If the fact that you like to mountain climb has nothing to do with your brand, leave the photos and diary of your last climb off the site. When you get a booking it's best to come to an agreement with the producer that they will plug your Web site on air and link to it from their own sites—thereby further building your brand and driving business your way.

If you are an idea person, or an expert in a particular field, publishing a book on your topic is one of the first ways to interest producers and to build a superstar platform. A newly published book is news in and of itself (more on pitching books in chapter four) and gives you credibility. Dr. Nicholas

Perricone, author of the best-selling books, *The Wrinkle Cure, The Perricone Prescription, The Perricone Promise,* and *The Perricone Weight-Loss Diet,* says that if you have a message it's best expressed in a book. "Then you have a purpose and something for journalists to report on," he adds. However, getting a book published is no simple matter for most people, and may be even more difficult than getting booked on a television show. You need a platform for that, too—so the whole process becomes something of a double-edged sword. There's not room enough in this book to discuss getting a book published, but there are some great resources available on the topic in bookstores and online.

 I have to tell you ...

Even in an age of technology, a business card is important

A business card can be slipped in with a mailing or handed to a producer (or anyone) when you are out and about. Always have cards with you—no excuses. Your business card should contain your name, address, land and mobile phone number, e-mail address, what you are (makeup artist, political consultant), Web site, and any logo or slogan. The information should be printed in clean, simple typeface. While cards can be attractive (they don't have to be just black and white) remember that combinations like white script type on a light blue background are hard to read.

Size and shape count, too. An oddly shaped card could be an attention-getter in the wrong way. They are annoying. Round, narrow, square, overly small or overly large cards can sometimes get tossed inadvertently or on purpose simply because they are too inconvenient for a producer to stick in her Rolodex (even though we all have databases on our Trios and BlackBerries, many of us still use old-fashioned card-filing systems too!). I can't tell you how many people have lost bookings because I bypassed them as I desperately looked for a last-minute guest because of a confusing (or discarded) card. Keep your card elegant, simple, clear, and fairly traditional—and don't forget to keep them in your wallet or purse!

Marta

Dr. Perricone says he appeared on television as a dermatologist before he wrote his first book. "But after *The Wrinkle Cure* was released, it gave me so much more of an opportunity and so many other ideas to discuss other than simple skin care. There are a lot of dermatologists out there with books but I was talking about a new science, which at the time was very controversial (the concept of beauty obtained from the inside out). Now, of course, it is established and the naysayers have gone back into the woodwork," he explains. At the time the controversy helped, especially since it was being argued in a book put out by a reputable publisher.

Although the book is very good, and would have probably sold well enough without help from television, the media helped boost the book's profile to astronomical heights. "TV is the most important because it lets you reach so many people. You do not get to be a *New York Times* best seller without it," says Dr. Perricone.

Offering your services as a guest speaker to clubs and organizations and writing letters to the editor or articles for a magazine or newspaper are other somewhat more accessible ways to build a platform and create awareness and interest in your message. From those outlets many a platform has been born. At first, you may have to offer your work for free—it is a small price to pay. Starting a blog or gaining an online audience on a service such as MySpace is another possibility—and many people have started wonderful careers and garnered a television audience because of these outlets. However, there are countless blogs and streaming video sites on the Web, and most of them are not very good. They are badly conceived, not very well written or filmed, or consist of personal rants and hissy fits that don't mean much to the general public—or all of the above. If you are going to take the time to create a blog or video to tell people about your ideas, remember that you are making a public statement, not creating a private scrapbook.

That said, a handful of people have been discovered via blogs and online video and gotten book deals, with TV not far behind. If you have a business idea, the Internet can be a powerful marketing and moneymaking tool. Aside from scouring the print media, producers also surf the Web looking for the latest thing.

Julie Powell became an Internet celebrity when she started a blog in 2004 that told of her yearlong mission to cook her way through Julia Child's *Mastering the Art of French Cooking*. The blog caught the attention of a publisher, it was expanded and put out as a best-selling book, and television appearances followed. She created a unique platform indeed! And it seems to be based on the author's sincere desire to write and cook.

Another Internet sensation is twenty-year-old Brooke Brodack of Holden, Massachusetts. She posted a range of videos starring herself on YouTube that have inspired an enthusiastic following. Ms. Brodack is a receptionist, but not long ago an executive at Carson Daly's development company made a deal with her to develop entertainment ideas for TV and the Web.

Supermarket Sweepstakes

 *Spotlight On:* Teri Gault

The Grocery Game

Teri Gault, a California mom, started an online service called The Grocery Game that connects shoppers with great supermarket deals. Teri hits all of our buttons: she has a great backstory, a fabulous platform, and a Web site business that backs it all up. Teri was a mom who wanted to find a way to feed her family economically, and what she discovered, she realized, could benefit other families as well. Her idea and her pitches center around her persona as someone who wants to save money but have a well-stocked pantry and a great life. Who doesn't want to do that? She is very relatable.

Teri got booked on the *Today* show to demonstrate the way The Grocery Game works—taking a crew to a grocery store. It worked—that appearance catapulted Teri's business and made her a millionaire. Her soon-to-be-published book is another benefit of being on TV. We sat down with her when she was visiting New York.

Starring You!: *What is the story behind The Grocery Game?*
Teri Gault: I had been saving money at the grocery store with coupons for years. I'm a wife and mother and am interested in feeding my family well but economically. I started The Grocery Game in my bedroom, and did not

know anything about the Internet. I realized you could match manufacturer's coupons with store sales and coupons and save a lot of money—if you knew how to track sale cycles. I built a free site to share this information with friends and it crashed! From day one, I knew it would be a great story and a great business. In fact, we have a cult following. I was literally rolling coins so I could afford to buy a business license. From day one the business took off —by the end of the first year, in February 2003, people started saying, When are you going to write a book? So now I am doing that, too. We now have seventy-three Grocery Game sale lists in fifty states and we are adding more all the time.

SY: *Who doesn't want to save money—but who has the time to track down sales and coupons? You solve two problems. Did you always see television as part of your business strategy?*

TG: Yes, from the beginning. I believe in the medium. It reaches our target market: women who want to save money. It's visual, as are groceries. There is no better way to see how The Grocery Game works than when you see the action and the drama at the register. Only television can deliver that. You can read about it all you want, but seeing it is amazing. And a segment on a talk show or morning news program is essentially a third-party advocate. **That's important because our story is so unusual and people are skeptical. Having that news reporter there with his or her objectivity is so important.** We do not do any advertising. PR is what works for us, especially since we are reaching out to women and they are the TV audience.

SY: *And you can actually go out to a store and show how it works?*

TG: Yes, that's essential. I am the face of the company, the founder. I better know how to play The Grocery Game! The setting is important, too. We do a whole lot better when we are in the grocery store as opposed to sitting in a studio with groceries spread out in front of the host and me. In a store, viewers get to see the groceries being scanned and the receipt come out.

For example, my *Today* show appearance was very dramatic. The producers found a woman who was very skeptical about the game so I showed her how it worked at the computer. She still wasn't sure, and she was very intelligent, and I thought, Good! Let's go to the store now. That was the segment. She had to pay for the groceries with her own money. I was putting all sorts of brand-name items in her cart, and she was worried about how she was going to pay. When we checked out, we bought $235 for $45. They would not let her look at the register until the end, and the reaction—her expressions saying *WHAT?!*—was priceless. And she started to cry.

SY: *And I imagine that each demonstration becomes part of your story and grows your platform?*

TG: Yes, I am not only the woman behind The Grocery Game. I am branding myself as a grocery store expert. Shows that have me on to talk about grocery trends in general, and not about The Grocery Game per se, are important. Those segments may not bump sales for the business, but it gets my name out there over and over again, as an authority. Groceries and grocery stores are my core topic.

SY: *How did you formulate your first pitch?*

TG: I used to be a grant writer so I knew how to write a press release. I called every local news show that had five and eleven o'clock shows. February is one of the sweeps months (*SY note: sweeps are four periods used for measuring television audiences to determine advertising rates, and are normally held during February, May, July, and November*), and so I started contacting them in January about doing February segments. Actually, even that was a little late. I should have been doing it in November if I wanted to get booked during sweeps. I faxed, called, and e-mailed and got three segments on different channels.

SY: *Since you might have been unknown to the producers, how did you pitch yourself?*

TG: My pitch was a headline: "Shoppers Saving Hundreds of Dollars in LA." I called the news desk and said, 'I have a great story for your sweeps,' and some would not talk to me. I went in with the same attitude I had when I went in for casting calls as an actress. I just kept trying. I knew it worked, because I had proof.

SY: *That was your platform. Your business worked.*

TG: Yes, groceries are an expense and I knew how to reduce it. I knew that if one show said yes, that would get the ball rolling. Because viewers will learn something from me whether they sign up for my Web site or not.

SY: *The Grocery Game is your business, but the bigger picture is seeing you as an expert, with a broader platform than The Grocery Game then?*

TG: Of course, general segments that concern your topic build your credibility. **You cannot keep going back to do the same story over and over.** We come up with different pitches. Because I am now seen as an expert on saving money, I can talk about all kinds of related topics, including the business I run. I have appeared with Shepard Smith on *The Fox Report* on the heels of a *Today* show, and I have been on other business shows and featured in *Entrepreneur* magazine and *Money* magazine articles.

It's All About You

Here's an assignment: Take out a sheet of paper or sit down at your computer and write out your personal story or biography—it does not have to be long, just authentic and heartfelt. If you have trouble, start by taking a look at your résumé and then write it out as paragraphs instead of the usual bullet points. There are great examples to inspire you—just take a look at the professional biographies of any of the guests and on-air people mentioned in this book (most are easily available on the Internet—a quick Google search will bring you to them).

A paragraph or a couple of pages is probably enough. Don't overthink it. Just tell the truth. Where did you come from? What drives your interest or expertise? Once you have it down you can refer to it when crafting pitches or in preparation to talk to or meet with a producer. There is power in the personal. You may very well be surprised what you find when you write your biography—ideas and angles always occur to you that hadn't before you sat down to really think about it.

When you're done, make a list of ten topics you can talk with authority about—this list is always evolving as you develop your brand and message. In fact, it's just the beginning.

Finally, remember that all the things you do and present to the world are an opportunity to express your message and platform—from business cards to blogs, e-mails to a letter to the editor of your local paper. Every time you meet someone new could be the opportunity you are looking for. Take every chance to express yourself in the best possible way. We've met people who turned out to be amazing TV guests in a lot of different places—parties, at the beach, on vacation . . . the next person *you* meet could be a producer. Be prepared!

 It's a Wrap

- You need a platform that bolsters your expertise and uniqueness.

- Your backstory is what makes you relatable to the audience.

- Know your stuff—if you say you're an expert, act like one.

- Make sure all business cards, Web sites, and other material are clear, concise, and elegant.

- Let your passion show—it's your most convincing calling card.

Chapter 3

Know the Shows!

It didn't take much imagination to name this chapter—it happens to be the exact phrase every producer we know, ourselves included, immediately shouts out when asked, "What's the number-one piece of advice you can give someone who wants to get booked on a television show?" If you start pitching shows before making sure that they book the kind of segments or expertise you're offering, your days in TV won't be numbered, they will be nonexistent. **The most insulting thing you can do is propose an idea that is irrelevant to a particular show—the producer will dismiss you in less than fifteen seconds.** And he or she will be annoyed to boot.

Recently we went to a very glitzy launch party for a household product from one of the biggest home product manufacturers *in the world*. It shows just how out of touch corporate America is with how they can use TV. Some companies spend thousands of dollars to rent a fancy loft space, provide fancy food and drink, and hire a PR firm. Yet when we met the number-two PR person at the firm, he was not at all ashamed to tell us he had no idea what was on daytime TV and that he never watched it. It was a total turn-off for us, and an embarrassment to the company. We were dumbfounded. It should be a requirement that someone in a company is watching TV and reports on what's happening. That should be a job—get an intern to do it! And all PR people should have televisions *turned on* in their offices.

Oh, and lesson number one of the Know the Shows class: get the *names* of the show and the host right. Even some pros get it wrong, which we find shocking. One of our favorite examples of that faux pas is when a publicist called Terence at *The Rosie O'Donnell Show* one day and said, "I have a fantastic segment idea for Roseanne." "Great!" came T's reply. "You better give Rosanne a call right away—I have to go; I'm producing Rosie's show."

Veteran producer Julie Cooper, currently the coordinating producer of *Wife Swap* and a former producer at *The View, Extreme Makeover,* and many other shows, says there is nothing worse than a person, especially a public relations professional, who not only doesn't know the show, but freely admits it. "It doesn't make sense to me. A publicist will call and say, 'I have never seen your show and I don't have a TV in my office, but I want to tell you about my client, because I think you'll be interested in her.'" Anyone interested in getting booked on a show should be watching it—and if it is your profession to get people media bookings, you should have a television in your office. And it should be on."

Lee Schneller, producer of *E! Entertainment News*, concurs: "We get a million pitches for human-interest stories that have no celebrity angle whatsoever. One hundred percent of the time we say no to those pitches. It's entertainment news; all the stories have to be related to that. Demographics are important, too. *E! News* captures female viewers, aged eighteen to twenty-four. What would they be interested in?"

Lee brings up a good point. While there are slight nuances in the demographics of unscripted and informational shows, most are watched primarily by women, including the nightly network news. The *E! News* audience skews younger than *The View* and the nightly news, but women make up the majority of their audiences also. According to Neilsen Media Research, in 2006 twice as many women as men watched the morning news. About 4 million more women than men watched the evening news. The numbers for daytime television are even more dramatic. There are exceptions: sporting events and shows about military history are more popular with men. That means most pitches either have to have an appealing element for women or they have to be "gender neutral," at the very least, so both sexes will be interested in staying tuned.

Know as much about each show's potential audiences as you can so you pitch the right way to the right show, says Albert Lewitinn, senior broadcast producer of *Showbiz Tonight* on CNN. "That is key because if your audience is primarily in the Bible Belt, for example, there are ways to make yourself more appealing as a guest. Gay adoption is not going to get booked on a show in Alabama, general adoption would," he says.

Learn everything you can about shows' formats, audiences, types of guests the hosts like to chat with, and the topics they are most likely to cover. Adam Spiegelman, a segment producer for *Jimmy Kimmel Live*, says there are still some people who do not think there is a difference between an evening show and a daytime show. There is. "We get pitches about speed dating, cooking, and getting engaged. We always turn them down. We like unusual people and humor. And it has to have an edge, since we are a late-night show," he says.

The biggest mistake people make is sending the same pitch to every show, regardless of format or content, and to us, that's lazy. Once you understand the show's format and topic preferences (how-to, entertainment, or news/informational, for example), you can tailor your pitch to fit it. That's the good news: with a little thought almost any area of expertise can fit any show. We think it's important to understand a little "TV talk," too—being familiar with the language of television makes you a bit more sophisticated about the business in general. You'll feel more comfortable talking to a producer, even if you don't actually use any broadcasting terminology in an actual conversation. It's very similar to formulating your back-story—the details may never come up in conversation, but they give you a foundation. Remember, producers have big egos, and they want to know you are watching their show.

Stay Tuned

The first, best, and easiest way to get to know the shows is by watching them as an active viewer. We watch everything that comes out. TiVo is our best friend—we can review every show in minutes. Most of us watch TV passively, and by that we mean we just let whatever the show is wash over us without paying much attention to the nuances of the set, the timing of segments, and the specific language used by the host and guest. In the case of news and information shows, sometimes we listen while doing something else, such as folding laundry or writing an e-mail. We are not really giving what's on any *critical* appreciation.

Here's an assignment: Starting Monday, watch the 8 A.M. to 9 A.M. hour of one of the three morning *network* (ABC, NBC, or CBS) shows for five days. It does not matter which one you watch, whatever one you like. The 8 A.M. to 9 A.M. hour is one of the best for catching a wide variety of guests, since the first hour or, at the very least, the first half hour, of most morning shows is reserved for hard news topics that feature journalists and politicians.

Now, pay close attention and make a note of:

1. Every time a new segment is introduced and then executed during the hour.
2. How long each segment lasts.
3. The average length of each segment, and any that go much longer.
4. Topics that get the most segment time.
5. The number of questions the host asked the guest in each segment.
6. The approximate length of each answer.

Now think about:

1. How many visuals were involved with the segment?
2. Were segments in the studio, outside, or on location?
3. Did the guests stay on point? Did they ramble?
4. What do you think of the guests? Were they interesting, concise, and easy to listen to? Or were they nervous and vague?
5. What are the qualities you liked about the guests?
6. What are the things that turned you off about the guests?

7. What did you learn and how did you benefit?

Next, go through the same set of questions while watching a cable news show from 8 A.M. to 9 A.M. for a few days. You'll see distinct differences between them. Fox News and CNN cable, for example, are much more news oriented than the network morning shows. These cable shows are less likely than one of the network morning programs to have a segment about "great summer tanning solutions." However, the twenty-four-hour cable morning news shows may be more likely to spend longer on a single topic than their Big Three counterparts. *GMA, Today*, or *The Early Show* might give four to five minutes to a single topic, while CNBC or MSNBC might spring for seven or eight. Those few minutes can make a big difference to your message.

Use this same set of questions when watching any talk or guest-oriented show you come across or are interested in appearing on, including local shows. As we said earlier, a one-hour lifestyle show generally has opening and closing segments, and five seven-minute segments. Yet an evening talk show might have one guest for seven minutes with the rest of the time devoted to comedy skits or musical entertainment. Clearly, the same pitch is not going to be effective for all these different kinds of programs.

If you know the timing of segments and what kind of angle the show likes to take you'll be that much further ahead when it comes to crafting a segment idea. For example, if you see that the show you are targeting does mainly four-minute segments, and likes to include demonstrations, make sure your proposal reflects the time constraints and production preferences. Don't think four minutes is a lot of time? It's harder than you think to fill it with valuable information delivered in an enthusiastic manner (more on timing your presentation in chapter five).

Pay attention to regular features and recurring guests. Most guest-oriented shows have regular experts who cover certain topics for them. Generally these people have a contract or agreement with the show to make a certain number of appearances during the year. Who are they and what are their topics? For example, the *Today* show uses Bobbi Brown for most of their makeup segments. This doesn't mean you can never get a booking on *Today* if you are a makeup professional. It just means you are going to have to offer some tips, skills, or information that are different from what they already get from Bobbi Brown.

"*Today* also has about six regular fashion people," says Julie Cooper. "I cannot imagine that you would get booked to talk about fashion," she says. However, your fashion product may get a spot in a contributor's roundup—in that case send one of their fashion people your pitch and product and they may follow up on it.

Know what's happening on the shows. For example, during part of Tony Danza's daytime talk show run he was expecting a grandchild, and then the baby was born. All you needed to do to know this fact was *watch his show* a few times, since he enjoyed sharing his excitement over the impending birth at the start of every episode. If you had any information about being a grandparent, or about babies, pregnancy, or newborns, this would have been the perfect opportunity to pitch it to *The Tony Danza Show*'s producers. First, they would be flattered that you were paying attention to what the host was saying, and second, they would be predisposed to book a guest who had information that Tony was personally interested in learning about.

On the other hand, you also have to be conscious of what a host would *not* be interested in. "Tony would not do segments on Botox or cellulite cream," says the former human-interest producer on the show, Fran Brescia, who is now at *Martha*. "Come on—he's a man's man; he is not going to do beauty or makeovers." Despite that fact, Fran says she still received such pitches, usually from PR people. True, Tony's audience was primarily female, but the host's preferences shifted the topics to other, less "girls only" subjects, such as parenting, cooking, fitness, and family fun. We cannot stress enough that while demographic information in general is helpful, the only way you can find out the idiosyncrasies about a show is to watch it.

Think fast when you hear something that relates to your topic! If we were fitness instructors and wanted to get booked on *The Ellen DeGeneres* show because we love her (and we do) and we knew her audience of mainly women age twenty-five to fifty was exactly right for us, we would watch her show and listen very carefully for anything she said about sports or fitness. If we heard her say, "I don't know how to roller-skate," that would be our cue. We would look at each other and say if we owned a roller rink or made roller skates or were a roller skate expert we would be calling that show. That is the perfect chance for someone involved in roller-skating to get huge exposure. If we were an ice skate manufacturer and heard her say that, we would ship her enough skates for everyone in her audience and crew, *and* take her to the nearest rink for a demonstration. The producers would think, Wow, these people are paying attention! Let's give them a chance.

Keep up on what is happening in the news, films, and on popular series. For example, there was a great deal of excitement over the premiere of the film version of the best seller *The*

Devil Wears Prada. If you are a magazine person or a fashion expert, you could pitch yourself to the news shows as an expert who could comment on the realism of the movie or some other angle. If it is a smaller or local show that cannot book the author of the book or the principals from the movie, you might be an excellent alternative for them. If you are a forensic expert and you see something interesting on the season premiere of *CSI*, you might pitch yourself as a real-life example of what's happening on the show. Trend Web sites such as www.dailycandy.com, www.instyle.com, www.style.com, www.fashiondaily.com, and www.trendcentral.com are excellent sources for checking out the latest and greatest fashion, beauty, and pop culture must-haves of the moment.

If you have limited time and cannot devote a week to active viewing, tune in to a given show at least twice and do a little research. (We also have plenty of shows listed in the resource section and it's a great start.) The Internet is your best friend. *All* networks have Web sites that link to their individual offerings and "About the Show" sections. Read them! The degree of detail these descriptions offer varies from show to show, but at the very least you will get basic information about the show's format and host, including the correct spelling of his or her name. Often (but not always) the show's Web page also lists the executives and producers in charge and what the show covers. Most big shows, and all service shows, have a direct "be a guest on the show link," and you can click and pitch yourself. **Some of Terence's all-time favorite guests were those who wrote in to the show, not those whom he scouted.** Some show sites offer details on past and upcoming guests and segments—another acceptable alternative to getting a handle on topics and guests if you can't devote a lot of time to watching the show.

I have to tell you …

There is a language of television

You don't have to learn all the lingo and terminology of television, but it's helpful to know an assortment of words and what they mean. What follows is an assortment of some key terms and a good start to get you thinking and talking like a pro!

- **Audience:** The number of homes or people tuning in to a particular show.

- **B-roll:** Supporting video and images used to visually enhance an interview or narration.

- **Chyron:** A piece of equipment that allows video editors to insert text and graphics over an image on-screen—such as your name, the title of your book, your brand, your product, or your Web site address. **It's very important to your growth to make sure your chyron is correct.**

- **Dayparts:** How the television day is broken down. This is important because shows in particular dayparts do not usually compete with one another. In other words, you could be on an early-morning show and a daytime show on the same day, talking about the same thing, and the producers of these shows do not see it as a conflict:

  - Early Morning (EM): 5 A.M.–9 A.M. (CST)

  - Daytime: 9 A.M.–4 P.M.

  - Early Fringe (EF)/ Early News (EN): 4 P.M.–6 P.M.

  - Prime Access (PA): 6 P.M.–7 P.M.

  - Prime Time: 7 P.M.–10 P.M.

  - Late News (LN): 10 P.M.–10:35 P.M.

  - Late Fringe (LF): 10:35 P.M.–1 A.M.

  - Overnight: 1 A.M.–5 A.M.

- **Demographics:** The general makeup of the greatest audience for a particular show, including age range, gender, employment status, and even education and region of the country where they live. For example, most viewers for a daytime cooking show might be primarily women, age thirty-five–fifty-five, college educated, and live in the South.

- **Endless Content:** This is a somewhat new phrase that refers to a talent, show, or segment idea that has applications across many media platforms. For example, a show or segment about dating might be considered to have "endless content" because there could be additional information on a Web site, messages about dating related to the show could be sent to viewers' mobile phones, and books and magazine articles could result from the show as well. A concept that lends itself to endless content is the golden key to success.

- **Interstitial:** In television, this is the content in between programs that is neither an ad nor a full-length program. A good example of a TV interstitial is TBS's "Movie Makeover," which is a self-contained segment between the movie's being broadcast and advertisements.

- **O&O:** This is "owned and operated" and refers to local affiliate stations of a larger network. For example, a local channel in Dallas, Texas, or Portland, Maine, might be owned and operated by CBS.

- **Product placement:** When an advertiser pays for a specific product to be seamlessly integrated into the body of a show.

- **Promo:** A short, sometimes fifteen- or twenty-second spot previewing an upcoming show. A good example are the promos for the *Late Show with David Letterman*, which are put together literally minutes after the show tapes earlier in the evening, and are shown on CBS during prime time.

- **Rating Point:** The percent of the total available target audience that any given television show delivered to advertisers.

- **Reach:** The percent of the target audience that will watch a show at least one time.

- **Segment:** A section of a magazine, talk, or news format show devoted to a single subject, story, or guest.

- **Sizzle clip:** A very short, five- or ten-minute version of a proposed television show, showing its best or most exciting elements, the talent, and the basic premise or narrative.

- **Sound bite:** A concise statement that expresses a complete thought, idea, or concept crisply and economically.

- **Sponsored segment:** A segment of an informational or magazine format show that was paid for by a particular advertiser or organization because it has some connection to what is being discussed (favorably) in the segment. You can always tell a sponsored segment because an announcement before and after the segment runs will say something like "This portion of the program was brought to you by . . ." The Federal Communications Commission (FCC) mandates such disclosure.

- **Sweeps:** Several times during the year, a company called Nielsen Media Research measures television viewer markets to created ratings—hence *Nielsen ratings*, a term you have heard before. Shows use these ratings in part to determine their advertising rates. The better the rating, the more the show can charge for advertising on it. Nielsen collects demographic viewing data from sample homes in every 1 of the 210 TV markets in the country. Each home in the sample maintains a viewing diary for a week, noting what every person in their home watched. Many are paper diaries, but Nielsen has begun to supply some markets with electronic devices that track viewing habits.

The research firm says the word *sweeps* originated because they collect data (they sweep it up) for four weeks from four parts of the country: the Northeast, the South, the Midwest and the West. Standard sweeps months are November, February, May, and July. Clients such as advertisers and networks buy the results from Nielsen. Advertisers use it to make decisions about what products or services to advertise during what shows, and networks use it to make programming decisions (and to set ad rates). Check out Nielsen's Web site to find our current sweeps dates: www.nielsenmedia.com/sweeps.html.

- **Talent:** The host or star or cast members of a television show.

Marta

Variety Show!

There are several different kinds of programs on television—and not all of them use on-air guests. There are three broad categories of shows:

1. Scripted
2. Unscripted
3. Informational

Scripted: Soap operas and crime, legal, medical, and relationship dramas (think *As the World Turns, CSI, Law & Order, Desperate Housewives,* and *The OC*) are known as *scripted* shows. Actors follow scripts on these shows, of course, but many use expert consultants behind the scenes. *ER,* for example, employs emergency room nurses to advise the show's writers on realistic details and jargon used in emergency medical care, including the correct pronunciation of medical terms. Shows like *Law & Order* and *CSI* use policemen, lawyers, and forensic scientists to help formulate believable plots and credible scenarios and to integrate legal and scientific facts into the scripts. (For example, when the ADA on *Law & Order* references obscure case law or Gil Grissom of *CSI* casually tosses out multisyllabic insect names.) Situation comedies, miniseries, and television movies might also use experts behind the scenes, but it is less common and depends on the subject matter as to whether the show needs an expert consultant.

Getting a gig as a behind-the-scenes adviser on your favorite crime drama or medical series is not impossible, but it's quite different from building your reputation as an on-air expert. You need an agent to pitch your services to such shows, which is unnecessary when pitching ideas to *unscripted* and *informational* shows, which we're mainly focused on in this book (we do include a "behind the scenes" roundup in chapter six).

Unscripted: Talk and variety shows fall under this category. Shows such as *The View, Ellen, Oprah, The Tonight Show with Jay Leno, Late Show with David Letterman*, and *Jimmy Kimmel Live* are all considered unscripted. The paradox of unscripted shows is, of course, that they are scripted to a great degree. The host's opening remarks or monologue is written, all the segments are preplanned, and in many cases the conversation the hosts have with their guests are written out line by line. Whatever the case, all parties certainly know what topics will be discussed beforehand.

Reality shows such as *American Idol, Project Runway,* and *Extreme Makeover: Home Edition* are also considered unscripted. Check out our interview with one of the top reality producers in this chapter, Denise Cramsey, and the "Spotlight On" *American Idol* runner-up Constantine Maroulis. Both give you an insider's look at this unique but now ubiquitous sector of television (remember that a reality show appearance isn't the easiest route to lasting recognition, but it can certainly be an effective one).

Informational: Often these are either news-oriented or they offer how-to or lifestyle content, and they are usually formatted "magazine" style, which means they have a set number of segments per episode or are devoted to single subjects, such as a cooking show or a documentary. This broad category, which depends largely on guests and experts to provide material, includes everything from the *Today* show, *Entertainment Tonight, Extra,* and *20/20* to *Paula's Home Cooking* and *Forensic Files.* Shows like *Today* and the evening news are live; documentaries, news features (like those on CNN), and lifestyle shows are often taped.

Unscripted and informational programs offer you the most booking opportunities. We break these two categories down even further, and it's worth reviewing them so you can determine which formats are most appropriate for your skills. It's also important to understand the detailed distinctions in terms of pitching. A taped syndicated show is going to be more interested in "evergreen" topics that don't date than newsier items that might be time sensitive. Shows such as *GMA, The Early Show, Entertainment Tonight,* and *Extra,* which are shown live five days a week, are naturally going to be more interested in trends and segments related to what is going on in the daily news. Your pitch has to keep these factors in mind.

First, there are three sources for shows:

1. **Network:** *60 Minutes* and *Today* are examples of programs produced, owned, and shown by a particular network. A show like *CSI* is a network show but an outside production company creates it. Syndication rights to dramas and comedies are often sold to a cable or independent station after the show has been on for a while (the number of years it takes for a show to go into syndication has decreased over the past few years).

2. **Syndicated original:** *Ellen, Oprah, The Tyra Banks Show*, and *Regis and Kelly* fall into this group. These daytime shows could be on any network in different regions of the country (NBC might show *Ellen* in one market and CBS might be showing it in another part of the country), but they are often owned and produced by a major network such as Buena Vista, Warner Bros., or Universal and are made specifically to be sold into syndication. This gives the network an opportunity to find the right audience and time slot for the show in various markets. Some of these shows, such as *Ellen* and *Regis and Kelly,* focus on celebrity guests but they also feature human interest and lifestyle segments.

3. **Cable:** E! Entertainment, HGTV, the Food Network, Bravo, Lifetime, A&E, Style Network, and Oxygen outsource the majority of their shows or create joint ventures with production companies to produce proprietary programming. FOX, CNN, MSNBC, and ESPN create their own shows. E! does a mixture of in-house production, out-of-house production, and acquisition (when a network purchases a fully completed program, which has usually but not always aired elsewhere first). Each of their shows have teams of producers, and they either work for the network (E!, MSNBC, etc.) or the pro-

duction company that creates the show (HGTV, Bravo). There are cable networks popping up all the time, and since they are starting out and creating lots of new shows, they can't book guests fast enough, so cable represents tremendous media opportunities for all sorts of experts. Watch the show and check its Web site. Most cable networks do a lot of shows with the same production companies, and they are the ones you need to call or contact to get booked.

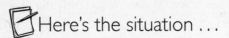

Here's the situation ...

Some daily talk shows take breaks in their shooting schedules.

It's called summer hiatus. For example, *Ellen, Oprah,* and *The Maury Povich Show* go on hiatus in the summer, while *Regis and Kelly* and *The View* keep on taping. If you want to pitch a show, make sure they are actually taping it. A skeleton crew is around during hiatus times, but they are generally not listening to pitches. The first couple of weeks of a new season are nuts, and that is also not the best time to pitch if you are an unknown. You can find out the schedule by calling or looking at the Web site. Check *TV Guide* to see if a show is being repeated for several days or weeks. If it is, it's on hiatus. Better yet, if you have TiVo, set it to record only new shows. It will not record a repeat so you can figure out if it is on hiatus! (You can maybe even write off your TiVo as a business expense—we do!)

Terence

Unscripted and informational shows can also be broken down into distinctive genres:

1. **Morning network news:** The big three are *Today, Good Morning America,* and *The Early Show*. These shows have several segments. The first hour is usually hard news–oriented and covers breaking news and stories that are related to big national stories, such as the war in Iraq, natural disasters, and elections. The second hour normally has "softer" stories. "Morning TV is the most powerful thing on earth. If there is a true connection to the person sitting across from you, you reach viewers," says Diane Sawyer, coanchor of *Good Morning America*.

2. **Nightly national news:** These shows primarily feature hard news, although evening network news programs also have human-interest stories and the "cute close" (the adorable pet story or other feel-good segment) as breaking news allows. They also call on experts to discuss current events. For example, if the president has a heart attack every news program would likely have a cardiologist on to discuss the medical aspects of the story, such as the kinds of treatments available, recovery time, and so on. They might also have a segment on what the rest of us can do to avoid a heart attack.

3. **Local network news:** Local network affiliates (a regional station owned by a network) may also have morning shows that replace one or more of the two to three hours the morning shows' schedule or that start an hour or so earlier. Local network stations often have daytime and early evening news and talk- or magazine-format shows eager for guests and segment ideas with regional appeal.

4. **News magazine:** *Primetime Live, Dateline, 48 Hours Mystery, 20/20,* and *60 Minutes* are examples of the news magazine. These shows generally pull stories from the news. Sometimes they cover unusual crimes, high-profile trials,

medical mysteries, or social trends. They are also interested in human-interest topics and their segments are story driven, meaning they use the same narrative techniques as a scripted drama uses. They often use experts or authors to provide commentary or a point of view on whatever subject they are reporting on.

5. **Magazine lifestyle:** These shows model themselves on the organization of a magazine, combining regular departments and feature stories. *Entertainment Tonight, Access Hollywood, Inside Edition, The Insider,* and *Extra* are examples. In other words, they offer multiple segments sometimes centered on a theme—like a magazine—instead of a single full story. Half-hour shows usually have four segments and one-hour shows have seven. They often use expert guests.

6. **Service:** *B. Smith with Style, Next Door with Katie Brown, Martha,* and any number of courtroom shows (*Judge Hatchett, Judge Judy*) are considered "service" shows because they provide viewers with help or advice.

7. **Relationship talk:** *Dr. Phil, The Dr. Keith Ablow Show, Maury Povich, Jerry Springer,* and *The Montel Williams Show* are considered relationship shows—they are all the same but in degrees. *Oprah* and *Tyra Banks* are talk variety, but can also be considered to be in this category. Obviously the demographics are slightly different for *Jerry Springer* as compared to *Dr. Phil,* but they are all essentially examining relationships and trying to come to conclusions about relationship issues (brawls and flying cameras notwithstanding!).

8. **Talk variety:** *Ellen, Rachael Ray, The Morning Show with Mike and Juliet, Oprah, David Letterman, Tonight Show with Jay Leno, Late Night with Conan O'Brien, Jimmy Kimmel Live,* and *The Late Late Show with Craig Ferguson* are good

examples (although David Letterman has said in interviews that he considers his show a comedy show with guests). When you are dealing with shows that depend on celebrities it is easier to get booked on one that is starting out and still working on finding an audience. They may not yet have the clout to book A-list stars and they do need guests.

 I have to tell you ...

Real people sometimes have an edge over publicists

Experts tell us that Oprah's show is less inclined to accept pitches from publicists; they prefer to hear directly from the person.

Marta

9. **Reality:** A reality show is generally characterized by a group of people solving problems or reaching a goal in some challenging situation. The idea is that they present "real" people in "real" situations—even though the shows are all professionally and carefully produced and edited to create an interesting and often humorous narrative. They often have a competitive component, such as *Survivor, Wife Swap, American Idol, Project Runway, America's Next Top Model, The Next Food Network Star,* and *Fear Factor.* Shows like *Extreme Makeover: Home Edition* and *A Baby Story* do not have a competition per se, but they do explore difficult or compelling personal circumstances of the show's subject. Game shows, some documentaries, dating shows, and competitive lifestyle shows or those that chronicle a real person's design/lifestyle efforts (such as *Trading*

Spaces, Weekend Warriors, Clean Sweep, and *Designed to Sell*)
also fall into the reality bucket. There are even celebrity reality
shows—*Circus of the Stars* was one of the originals and *Dancing with the Stars* was a recent surprise hit.

Reality shows have proliferated in recent years and now
it seems every network, cable station, and syndicator has at
least one on their menu. We noticed recently that the Fine
Living network was searching for a golfer to star in a golf
reality show. Since the reality show's stock and trade is casting real people, you would think your chances of getting on
one is better than getting booked on a morning news show.
Not necessarily. The competition for the most popular reality
shows is fierce. If you have ever stood in a blocks-long line to
try out for the first round of *American Idol,* you know what
we mean.

On the other hand, there are so many reality show opportunities that you could try out for more than one (check out
our chat with *American Idol* runner-up Constantine, who was
also a contestant on the dating reality show *Elimidate*). Some
of the morning news programs have their own mini reality
shows, such as talent contests that run over several weeks,
and cable channels such as the Food Network and HGTV
have contests to find new show hosts. So now you can actually search for the right reality show for your talent or skills
and you will probably find one. Being on a reality show can
help your career. Elisabeth Hasselbeck and Kelly Clarkson are
great examples. And you do not even have to win! Elisabeth
was a *Survivor* runner-up, and she is now the youngest host
of *The View*.

After seeing Elisabeth appear on *Rosie* and mention that
she loves fashion after being thrown off the island—a segment

Terence produced—Marta pegged her to be the host of a fashion reality program called *The Look for Less*. She has such a great personality and wonderful energy so she was the perfect fit. Elisabeth is a natural for TV.

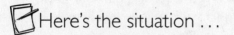

Here's the situation ...

Your best chance to get booked on a show if you are just starting out is between sweeps periods.

TV producers plan special bookings/events during sweeps periods (February, May, July, and November). They also premiere their seasons in September and usually have special holiday bookings during December. Therefore, unless you fit into their special plans and themes, **you have a better chance getting booked during the remaining months—January, March, April, and October—when they're desperately looking for good ideas.**

Terence

Producers and agents watch reality shows as if they were casting calls. So in that sense they *could* be a showcase for your talents as a host or performer . . . if you're good. The down side is that stories like Elisabeth's and Kelly Clarkson's are rare. Think about all the hundreds of people who have had their fifteen minutes of fame on a reality show who you never hear about. Most do not get discovered, and they go back to their normal lives. If you're smart, you can use your experience on reality TV as a springboard to enhance your existing career. That's what natural food chef Bethenny Frankel did after taking the runner-up spot on Martha Stewart's version of *The Apprentice*.

Even before Bethenny competed in the show, she had cooked for such high-profile clients as Mariska Hargitay; Kathy, Paris, and Nikki Hilton; Alicia Silverstone, Michael J. Fox; and several clients of the nutritionist to the stars Oz Garcia. "**I used the tiny seed of the show to bust the door wide open.** Without even close comparison, I've gotten infinitely more press than any of the other fifteen contestants, including the winner—and I did it without a publicist: *OK!* magazine twice, *People,* the *New York Post, Us Weekly, VegNews,* Martha's daytime show, *The Howard Stern Show,* and many others," she says.

Appearing on a reality show was simply an extension of Bethenny's efforts to become well known in her field. She combined the contacts she made on the show with her natural ability to walk up to anyone and strike up a conversation. "On the day of the finale, I walked straight up to Bill Clinton, asked him to touch me for good luck, we chatted, and then I informed him that he had spinach in his teeth. Not long ago, I talked to Kelly Ripa and Brooke Shields about cooking for them. I never let opportunities slip away."

That is really the point of being on reality TV—it is part of the means to your ends. It is another opportunity. Bethenny says that to make the most of a reality show, you have to have something interesting and marketable behind you. "I'm a natural foods chef and building myself as a brand. A reality show was a perfect vehicle for me. You can use the show to get you in doors, but drop it right there. People don't respect reality contestants. In the press now I'm known as a celebrity natural foods chef and *never* as a reality star. If I could have afforded it, I would have hired a publicist but I would instruct them to market my skills and me, and not the show."

The Reality of It All

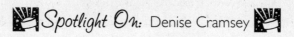 *Spotlight On:* Denise Cramsey

We sat down with our colleague Denise Cramsey to get her perspective on the reality show business. Terence has worked with Denise, and she is one of the best in the business. In fact, she is a veteran of the genre, having produced *Trading Spaces, A Baby Story, A Wedding Story, Medical Detectives, Gimme Shelter, House Wars, Manhunt: The Search for America's Most Gorgeous Male Model,* and now is co–executive producer of the popular *Extreme Makeover: Home Edition.* The show pairs owners of homes badly in need of repair with several opinionated designers, who help revamp the home and the homeowners' lives. The show's successful first season garnered an Emmy nomination for Outstanding Reality Program. In its second season it won the People's Choice Award for Favorite Reality Show/Makeover and the Family Television Award for Best Alternative/Reality Program. It's also a certified ratings hit for ABC.

Starring You!: Denise, what do you look for when reviewing the tapes potential reality show participants send in?

Denise Cramsey: I look for people who have great per-sonalities, who are able to talk and be humorous and show their personality, who can speak clearly, and who get their points across and appear to be having fun on camera.

SY: What is the process for getting pegged for a reality show?

DC: There is lots of preinterviewing and gathering of

information. Potential candidates fill out an application and talk to a lot of people [from the show]. But I think all casting, whether it is for professional talent or real people, comes down to a gut feeling about whether the person is sincere and they are going to be able to appear well on TV.

SY: *What about the personal story shows you worked on, like* A Baby Story *and* A Wedding Story? *How do you find people and what's the motivation for appearing?*

DC: There will always be shows like that—viewers find them compelling as stories and helpful if they are in similar situations. In a case like that, people send in their stories for consideration. In a couple of cases we contacted midwives and OBs and asked for wonderful families. By and large the viewers are writing in. Those kinds of shows are extremely stressful and emotional for the participants. That is something to keep in mind. The person really has to want to do it. It's not something you can talk someone into doing because it is extremely invasive and personal. I think the motivation in some cases with *A Baby Story* is that the moms want to share their experiences with others, especially if it concerns a multiple birth or a difficult pregnancy in some way, so viewers can be inspired or learn something.

Mostly, though, people want to capture that moment in their lives in the most professional way. *A Wedding Story* is the highest end wedding video you can get. For that show we looked for brides and grooms who had sincerity and true commitment to each other. It would not be a couple who met last week and wanted to elope. For *Wedding Story* to work you had to like the people and get behind them and root for them. We looked for couples who had to overcome some odds in their love, whether it be they were separated by distance or tragedy or a strange twist of fate.

SY: *What is the biggest pitfall potential reality candidates face?*
DC: There are two things people have to remember. No one becomes a star simply because they have been on a reality show. Look at Trista and Ryan—arguably the biggest and most talked-about reality personalities. *(SY! note: Trista and Ryan met on* The Bachelorette, *inspired after popular Trista lost out to another woman on the ABC reality show* The Bachelor.*)* They are back to their normal lives. A lot of people on competition shows think they are going to get lucky and get their big break—the country is fascinated for fifteen minutes and then they are not. So if you are selected for a show, make sure your expectations are reasonable.

The second thing people have to know is that there is no down time on a reality show. You don't get to say, Don't shoot me now. When you open up your life and want to be a part of this—it means you lose control of it for that show period. It can be great fun and an adventure, and it can also be stressful. That's what makes it reality. I have never had anyone removed from a show but certainly I know of situations like that on other programs. On *Baby Story* we had a couple who said, You have to leave, but we didn't. We have invested time and money and resources and we have to see it through to the end. We make that clear contractually from the beginning.

SY: *How can someone tell if they have what it takes to be a great reality show participant?*

DC: It is an intangible "it." Think of it in terms of your own life if you want to be on a reality show—or any TV show. Ask yourself, When I walk into a room do people notice? Do I make an immediate impression? It's not about being loud or obnoxious. It's charisma. The best reality TV candidates are the ones who have *presence.* If you don't have that seek another way. If you are not sure, ask your friends to answer this question honestly: "When I walk into a room do you notice me?" If they say yes, you are good to go.

SY: *What's the advice you dispense most often?*

DC: I tell everyone: Be yourself. The shooting of a reality show or any production requires long hours. The work is hard, and if you are trying to portray a character you will never be able to keep up that pretense. Being true to yourself is what is going to stand you in good stead throughout the production.

Spotlight On: Constantine Maroulis

So what is appearing on the *hottest* reality show and then ending up on the pages of *Us Weekly* really like—from a contestant's perspective? We sat down with *American Idol* runner-up Constantine Maroulis. Even though he did not win the *Idol* competition, Constantine knows firsthand how being on a reality show can make you a star, whether you win or not. He has formed a fan base and extended his musical career greatly—including a stint on Broadway in *The Wedding Singer*. We talked to him about being on *American Idol*, not winning, and what happened afterward.

Constantine grew up in Bay Ridge, Brooklyn, New York. He took a break from performing with his band, Pray for the Soul of Betty, to compete in the fourth season of *American Idol*, making it to the final six contestants. Before competing on the show he trained at the Boston Conservatory of Music and played the role of Roger in the international touring company of *Rent*. When he was finally voted off the show on April 27, 2005, his final song was a rendition of Nickelback's "How You Remind Me."

American Idol was not Constantine's first experience with the reality genre. He was at Juilliard studying singing when he tried out for and Terence produced him on *Elimidate*. He even won the date! Now he has signed a deal with Disney to develop and host a show and he has his first post-*Idol* solo album coming out.

Constantine's story is a good example of not having to "win" to have success from a reality appearance. Yes, we acknowledge what Denise says about it not being a direct ticket to stardom, but if you get yourself out there and become part of what's happening in the culture your chances of success are certainly increased.

Starring You!: *You did not go out for* American Idol *as a lark or for fun. You were serious about it—tell us about that.*

CM: Yes. I like to think it is like any task. Performing is a job. You start at the bottom and you work your way up. I put myself through school at the Boston Conservatory of Music and earned a BFA in Musical Theater. I was classically trained. This prepared me for work in rock-and-roll bands and for off-Broadway. I did not think it was possible for a guy like me to get on *American Idol*, but then I saw Clay and Ruben and said, Okay, I will audition. Everyone knew I was there for business. I was serious but I also had fun.

SY: *Did you have a strategy?*

CM: What is funny is that I did not want to stand out. I had a bit of a following from being in *Rent* so I did not want people to see me fail. I kept a low profile and that resulted in being somewhat mysterious. I also did not look like anyone else. I am six four and I have long hair. Then the producers heard me speak and they realized I had a brain and could hold a conversation with them and discuss politics and current events. They knew that I was versatile. They put me in the rocker category and they could pit the southern rocker against me, the guy from New York. It brought a lot of excitement and credibility to the show because we were two pros competing against sixteen-year-olds from the mall. It expanded the show's audience. I was also very grateful for the opportunity to show my versatility outside of the rocker vibe, because you perform a variety of songs on that show.

SY: *What advice would you give to future talent reality show hopefuls?*

CM: First, people see right through you on TV. It does not lie. You can always tell when a contestant isn't being himself or herself. Also, behave in a professional manner. Be humble, accept criticism, and use what the judges and producers tell you in a constructive way. You need confidence. Do not lash out. Being defensive is bad. I also took the opportunity to develop relationships with the people on the show. I have incredible friendships with producers all over the place. You cannot let it get to you that the 40 million people are watching. You have fans literally overnight, and you have to stay grounded.

SY: *How about after the show's over? What happens when you go home?*

CM: I am after long-term success. So for me it is getting the right jobs and being careful about what I do. I did not put out an album right away. I don't want to jump the gun—I want it to be quality, and that requires time and thought. I did not want to be in the situation of all of a sudden thinking, Oh, I am an idol, and forget all about what I learned at the Williamstown Theatre Festival or in my years of school and professional training.

I have to be honest. We all want to win, but I am philosophical. I may have lost because I wanted to shake it up and be a little tongue in cheek and maybe it was too much irony for the show. It was meant to be this way. I am excited for the album to come out and excited about the TV show and being on Broadway. I am shy, even though I come across as being bold. The recognition can be overwhelming. I was at a big party last night after laying low for a while and everyone there went crazy. It's really cool for fans to see you up close. It's an awesome experience and for me to be in that position to affect people and sing and act, it's incredible.

SY: *What else does a performer who might want to use reality TV to help make his or her name have to think about?*

CM: You have to be conscious of all aspects of the business. Music especially is very disposable. Now that no one is buying records you really need to serve music in a new disposable way. It is a shame, actually. I hope we do not lose that part of the market but it is changing. I love records and reading liner notes. But you also have to keep up with what is going on in the culture and technology. That's a fact of life.

Constantine's advice is valuable for anyone appearing on TV or who wants to "star" in his or her own life—be humble and graciously and gratefully accept criticism from professionals. Stay up to date with what is happening in the wider world. Once you are confident about yourself, and what's available to you on television, you are ready to pitch. But not so fast . . . there's an art to pitching, and you need to perfect it.

 It's a Wrap

- Get to know the shows you want to pitch by watching them.
- Pay attention to the topics each show covers.
- Don't pitch a segment that does not fit the show.
- Leave producers with the impression that you are someone who understands their show.
- Be confident about what you have to offer.

Chapter 4

Perfect Pitch

There are four facts you should know about pitching:

1. You *do* stand a chance of having your pitch heard. Producers are always looking for fresh content and new faces. We watch every tape and read all e-mails and hand-delivered pitches that look interesting, hoping one will be "it."
2. It's much easier to contact the right person at a show than you think—just call the show and ask. Sounds obvious, but people rarely do it.
3. Producers don't have time to steal your ideas, so don't hold back. Keeping salient facts "secret" is a great way to be dismissed out of hand.
4. Getting booked on television is not about looks, it's about being a great talker, being fast on your feet, and having fabulous ideas.

If you are skeptical about these statements now, we'll convince you by the end of this chapter. It's not that we want to make it sound easy to get booked. It's just not as *complicated* as people think it is. We never said anything about easy.

Who Gets a Pitch?

Producers, segment producers, and bookers field pitches in most cases. They pitch their bosses (senior or executive producers) the ideas they like at weekly creative meetings. Sometimes producers also pitch the show host. For example, Rosie was very involved in segment planning and okayed almost every idea and guest.

Don't send a pitch to just any producer on a show. Target the right person. If you send a food pitch to the guy who books sports, he is not going to acknowledge it. And since you "got it wrong" he won't be interested in helping you by passing it along to the right person. Why should he do your job?

Magazine, lifestyle, and news shows generally have several producers or bookers covering specific areas. Their titles may not always tell the story. Depending on your topic, ask to speak to the producer who covers human interest, lifestyle, fashion, health, food, medical, finance, sports, and so on. Talent producers book celebrities and celebrity-related stories, so if you are pitching something that ties in with a celebrity ask for the talent booker.

Sometimes producers at smaller, local, or newer shows cover more than one topic; at bigger shows the producers can be precisely segmented. For example, there may be a producer who covers the opening monologue of the host, one who covers news-related topics, one who covers fashion, another who handles food, yet another who looks at human-interest stories, and so on. It depends on the size and scope of the show.

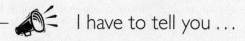 I have to tell you . . .

A TV show has many levels of producers

- **Executive producer** (EP) holds the head position on a TV show. He or she is ultimately responsible for the overall show, its creative content, the production staff, and the show's budget. The EP is hired by and reports to the executives of the network or production company. Sometimes several EPs with different strengths and skills are assigned to a show with diverse needs.

- A **Co-EP** reports to the EP and is often the "show runner" as well. Show runner is a hands-on position. He or she takes care of the nuts and bolts of the show's day-to-day operations—from making sure scripts are ready to assigning segments to producers.

- **Senior producers** report to the EP and co-EP. All producers report to them on their segments.

- **Talent producers** are sometimes called talent executives. They handle the booking of celebrities and experts and often produce celebrity and expert segments.

- **Producers** and segment producers report to senior producers. They field pitches, pitch them to the senior producer, and, if they get the go-ahead, they produce the resulting segments.

- **Bookers and talent bookers** field pitches and pass them off to a producer once they have gotten an okay. Not all shows use bookers, but some do. Bookers don't produce—producers may both produce and book. "Booker" is less used nowadays because it's a title that does not make a person eligible for an Emmy Award. The term is often changed to "talent producer" or "talent executive" so the person is eligible for an Emmy Award.

Marta

Most producers are young, and many of them are female (as are the viewers, which we talked about in chapter three). That's just the way it is so keep it in mind. That is not to say that you cannot get booked if you are talking about issues related to older people or men. On the contrary. The producer is filling segments that appeal to their audience, not themselves. But you still have to find a way to make the pitch relatable to them. You have to speak their language: hip, up to date, and down to earth.

While you can send a pitch to a reporter who develops his or her own stories (see our roundtable with local reporters, producers, and bookers on page 106), do not send a pitch to a host. Hosts do not book segments. "The chances of a host taking out a product that was sent to them, and talking about it on air, is about one in ten thousand," says *Wife Swap* producer Julie Cooper, who also worked on *The View*. "It doesn't happen." What does happen is that he either gives it to a producer, who does nothing because she is annoyed the pitch was not sent to her, or she puts it on the bottom of her pile, for the same reason. Or the host never opens it or looks at it, or if he does he might give it to his assistant as a gift.

So how do you find out which producer does what? Do some legwork. The best way is to call the show and ask. The receptionist is your best friend. Be nice to him or her. He or she will probably be a producer in a few years and will have a long memory. Recently we needed to find out who the music producers were on the network morning shows. We could have called any one of our colleagues to find out, but instead we decided to put our advice to the test and we cold-called just to see what would happen. Great news: we got the names at all three shows with no problem, even though we didn't use our connections.

The Art of the Pitch

Producers are busy, tired, overwhelmed, and are producing segments at the same time they are looking for new ones. Therefore we have no attention span. So make your lives easier by making our lives easier, and be succinct. Your idea should be conveyed in less than a page, and ideally in one paragraph. Think about it: how long should it take to express a concept for a segment that lasts only three to seven minutes? Think in terms of the "tease"—what would make you "stay tuned." When thinking about your pitch, fill in the blank after "coming up next . . ." Now read it out loud. Would you stick around for the commercial to be over?

Good Morning America producer Raina Seitel Gittlin says once when crashing a story for the next day (not unusual for a producer of a news program) she got a pitch: "I have Celebrity X, can you book them in two weeks?" That's a bad pitch. "Celebrities are great, but even they need a hook. I need to know what the celebrity wants to talk about. I don't have time to come up with the topic myself," she says. "And the timing the publicist wanted was cutting it really close." Raina asked the publicist to give her two or three sentences describing what her client wanted to talk about. "I got five sentences back. Better, but please follow directions. Get to the point in the first two sentences and you will be ahead of everyone who writes a page," she says.

Don't think Raina's advice doesn't apply to everyone. Even A-list PMK/HBH publicist Cindi Berger (who reps such A-listers as Sharon Stone and Rosie O'Donnell) says she has to be prepared and always keeps it short and direct—and this is a woman who can call Matt Lauer on his cell phone! "If you have someone's ear for a couple of minutes you want to say the words that help achieve your goal, whatever it is. You need to know your points. **I never take relationships for granted.** When you pick up the phone to call someone like Diane [Sawyer] or Matt [Lauer], you better know what you're talking about," she says.

Since you are using few words, they must be carefully chosen. And that's where many people get tripped up. For example, it's not enough to say, "Hi, I am a gardener and I want to talk about gardening." Who are you and why should we care? What do you know about gardening that can save me time and money or make my garden more beautiful? How about how to turn your backyard into a million-dollar oasis for pennies . . .

"Experts don't seem to realize that they have to follow the news, so they can say, 'I am the person you want to have because I can tag on to story X, Y, or Z . . . ,'" says Albert Lewitinn, senior broadcast producer of CNN's *Showbiz Tonight*. "That's what TV producers look for, especially on cable, where they are on twenty-four hours and they have a lot of spots to fill," he explains. Producers sit at meetings and ask, How are we going to cover the story today? They need people.

If you are a psychologist or a marriage or relationship counselor, a great way to pitch your expertise is to tie in to something that is happening in the news: you know what makes the "real" *Desperate Housewives* tick or why best friends sometimes fall in love with each other's spouses, and so on. Big movie premieres offer another tie-in opportunity. If you work in the magazine business, you could have talked about the "real" *Devil Wears Prada* editors. If you know something about penguins or Antarctica, you can discuss the mating habits depicted in the animated Robin Williams feature *Happy Feet*.

Everyone wants the real people story. Studio Web sites such

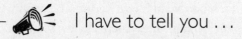 I have to tell you …

One of our favorite e-mail pitches was "Race to Erase 10 Years in 24 Hours" from publicist Tara Lowenberg.

What we love about it is that it has an intriguing hook and the pitch itself is very visual, to say the least (we used Tara's pitch on a daytime show). Instead of trying to pitch one client, Tara created a compelling narrative that *used* her three clients:

Subject: 3 ways to take 10 years off
your face in less than 24 hours
"Race to Erase"
Become 10 years younger in less than a day:

1. **Laser teeth bleaching**—dentist to the stars Dr. Marc Lowenberg

2. **Combination Hylaform and Cosmoderm/Cosmoplast injections**—filler for the face plumps lines and reduces wrinkles around the mouth and in the laugh lines. Celebrity dermatologist Dr. Ellen Gendler performs the procedures

3. **Makeup contour**—Target's cosmetic queen Sonia Kashuk demonstrates techniques that accentuate the positives and eliminate the negatives

Tara basically handed us a segment. That's a point we talk about in the next chapter: a dream guest delivers what they promise! I found a harried mom, had her drop her kids off at school, and before she picked them up in the afternoon, we took ten years off her life. Amazing!

Marta

as www.paramount.com, www.miramax.com, and www.fox-movies.com, and general film sites such as www.imdb.com provide information about recent or upcoming films; or you can also watch entertainment news shows or read the special movie edition of magazines like *Entertainment Weekly*.

If you're pitching your skill or expertise, package it around an idea or "news you can use." Television shows are not in the business of giving you a free commercial. In terms of time-sensitive stories, "the early bird catches the worm," says *Entertainment Tonight* co–executive producer Bradly Bessey. "Experts are usually a day late and a dollar short with ideas. If an expert wants to apply their knowledge to breaking stories, they have to come to me early. They are usually a day or two late. If an expert has an interest in getting on a daily news show like *ET*, they better check the news wires the night before and get to us early. I am in my office at 5 A.M. every morning when the senior staff is laying out the show, and I have already spoken to my partner, Linda [Bell Blue], at 4:15 A.M. We are always looking for 'next day' angles," he says.

Lee Schneller, who produces *E! Entertainment News*, says they, too, look for experts with inside information and a celebrity hook. "They should pitch the assignment desk because we are always looking for fresh news stories." Most of *Extra*'s segments are celebrity news driven, too, according to coordinating producer Rob Sheiffele. "But we are also looking for segments on unusual getaways or hot clubs. It is not necessarily a hard pitch, though, since I like to check it out personally and feel I have discovered it for the viewer." In that case, an exclusive pitch to Rob might be enticing. And if you say it is exclusive, make sure it really is. **There is nothing worse than getting an "exclusive" that was sent to every producer in town!**

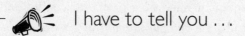 I have to tell you ...

Complicated, multipage press kits are often overlooked

We get numerous fancy, expensive press kits—and throw a lot of them away (unless we have specifically asked for it). It may actually hurt your chances of getting booked. Save your money and put your time into a creative pitch instead. If a producer asks for information in addition to the basic pitch, there is a very simple recipe for creating a great package:

- A one-paragraph idea—bullet points are great
- A one-page bio
- One natural-looking photograph, clearly marked with your name and contact infomation
- One TV reel, if available (see Terence's box on reels) with your name, profession, and contact infomation printed clearly on the tape's spine
- Press clippings or samples, if applicable

Every page of paper, every photo, and every reel in the kit *must* **have your name and phone number on it—your hotline number so a producer can get to you directly.** Combine these things in a simple folder and mail it or, better yet, have it hand delivered.

Marta

Paper or Processor?

Terence likes paper pitches, delivered creatively. It's old school but if done well, it's memorable and effective. Marta likes e-mail messages with bullet points—although a beautiful basket filled with an array of theme-driven products would impress her as a follow-up to an e-mail. There's no set formula. All producers have their own styles and preferences (that's why we talked to so many of our colleagues for this chapter).

The down side of a paper pitch is that it can get lost or never get opened. If you plan on mailing a pitch, consider having it hand delivered (apologies to the U.S. Post Office, but regular mail piles up and has a tendency not to get opened for days or even weeks). Anything that comes "special delivery" to a specific person is more prone to be read than something stuck in with junk mail. Be sure everything you send is clearly marked with your name and contact information. "People send me head shots with no name or number on it," says *Jimmy Kimmel Live* segment producer Adam Spiegelman, "and that is just not helpful."

Presentation counts. A creative, well-thought-out pitch delivered by hand is a provocative first sign to the producer that the segment will be good. If you are a chef, send a sample of your goodies right before lunch in a box with the name and logo of your restaurant, and your contact info, clearly marked on it. If you are a baker, put your pitch in a cookie jar and hand deliver it around 10:30 A.M. or 4 P.M., about the time that "office munchies" set in. Guilt them into calling you back. If someone sent us something homemade that obviously took some time, we would call him or her because we would feel bad if we ignored the effort.

Are you a kids' toys expert? Send your pitch on a board game. If you are a personal finance expert, tell us how you are going to save or make people money in five easy steps—and present it on the *Wall Street Journal*'s stock page or on play money. If you work for a hotel and are pitching a travel or vacation segment, make sure your pitch comes in your hotel's tote bag filled with cool travel or vacation stuff to make it really stand out (nothing too expensive, though, as many shows have policies against accepting gifts worth more than $50 or $100). When the producer gets back to his or her desk and sees any one of these pitches, he or she will pay attention!

Create a little intrigue or mystery. Tom's Cookies founder Tom Roach sent over a beautifully wrapped package of peanut butter banana cookies to *The Rosie O'Donnell Show* with a note that read, "If you eat these cookies you will have something in common with the president of the United States. Call me to find out what it is." The producer called and found out that the same cookies were served at President Clinton's inauguration! Voilà! Tom was booked on the show.

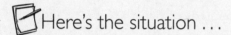Here's the situation ...

Events and holidays make great hooks

If you are pitching a major holiday (Christmas, Fourth of July) or event-centric (Election Day) idea, the general rule of thumb is to start contacting producers six weeks before it happens, and then follow up in three weeks. A great resource for quirky events and obscure holidays is *Chase's Calendar of Events*. Every TV producer uses this annual reference—it's our bloodline. It lists historical anniversaries, sporting events, celebrity birthdays, and regional festivals—even the phases of the moon. It's also expensive (about $65, including book and CD-ROM), but it is likely available at your public library. *Chase's* is exhaustive; less comprehensive and cheaper alternatives include *On This Date: A Day-by-Day Listing of Holidays, Birthdays and Historic Events and Special Days, Weeks and Months* ($17) and *The World Almanac and Book of Facts* ($12).

Terence

If you send an e-mail, which many producers prefer, make sure it is personalized. We delete ones with "Dear friend" or "Dear producer" greetings. It pays to put the person's name in the subject line along with the one-line idea. "Using my name is always good because it makes me think I may know the person," says *GMA*'s Raina Seitel Gittlin. "We get a lot of internal e-mail traffic because it is a daily news-sensitive show. If I see, 'Hey Raina, great pitch,' I won't skip it by mistake," she says.

"If I get six different ideas in one pitch, there is a sense that it is a mass mailing, so I won't use any of them," says Julie Cooper of *Wife Swap*. "You want to feel as if you are the only one getting the pitch, and the only one to book it."

Producers get hundreds of e-mails a week, and some of them automatically go directly into spam folders, or get marked as spam even though they make it into their in-boxes. The only way they can sort them is to assess the "subject" and "from" lines and delete what seems extraneous or dull. Since they may not recognize you from your "from" line (because they may not know who you are), the only thing they have to go by is the hook in your subject line. Make it good. Learn to think in short, provocative, and *active* bursts. Producers are trained to think that way and do not need long explanations.

Think in terms of what would get *you* not to change the channel when the host says, "When we come back, we're going to learn . . ." Be bold, be provocative, but be honest. Numbers are good, as are definitive solutions to problems or topical issues. Any of the following subject lines would get us to read an e-mail:

- 5 ways to get your man to propose by Valentine's Day
- How to look thinner for New Year's Eve (in 20 minutes)
- Create a dream wedding for less than $8000 (gown included!)
- 5 signs your bride is going to leave you at the altar
- 7 fast, painless ways to save $5000 by the end of the year
- Give up your morning latte for 12 months and afford a home of your own
- Turn your child into an A+ student by cutting out 10 minutes of TV a day
- Study shows colleges give students half an education: make sure your child is getting 100%
- Spend a weekend at Disney World for $50 a day

Pitches to Ditch

A bad pitch can ruin your chances of getting booked. Maybe not forever, and we know a lot of trial and error happens before you master any new skill. But it can derail you temporarily. One of our producer friends (we promised not to reveal his name) sent us the following e-mail pitch from a PR person, the result of a badly timed phone call made while he was taping a show! It's a classic example of a pitch that will never get airtime:

Hi Producer X:

> *Sorry to have caught you in the middle of the show! Wanted to run a quick idea by you for the week leading up to Mother's Day. We are very close to signing*

*with an up-and-coming celebrity chef who has a new
TV show that will be launching right around Mother's
Day timing. Because we are still working out a few
details I can't give you his name just yet, but I can tell
you that he's very young, very attractive, he has a great
vibe on camera and is definitely a rising star. He would
like to do an in-studio segment on preparing the perfect Mother's Day brunch for Mom. He would give tips
for husbands and kids on how to really make Mom
happy on her special morning with a great brunch.*

*Just wanted to get your initial feedback to see if
you'd be interested—let me know your thoughts!*

Thanks,
PR PERSON X

Strike 1—Calls during a live taping. Tip: Know when the
show tapes.

Strike 2—Pitches a guest but does not release his name. Is
she kidding?

Strike 3—The actual segment idea (preparing the perfect
Mother's Day brunch), buried at the end of the e-mail is also
flat and has no hook.

You're out!

On the other hand, there are *a lot* of *smart* publicists who
understand television, and you can learn a lot about how to
pitch from them (more about working with a publicist in chapter six). "A publicist I work with really gets TV. She almost
does my job, which I appreciate," says Fran Brescia, daytime
talk show producer. "She breaks the segment down, recom-

mends chyrons, and gives me almost more than I need. I know I can always call her, even at the last minute, and I get what I need," she says.

The publicist in question is Charly Rok, senior vice president of media at Lippe Taylor in New York, who cautions that while most producers love it when you hand them a segment, polished from top to bottom, a handful don't like it, and prefer simple pitches they can develop in-house. "The *Today* show would go ballistic if you tried to produce their segments," she says, "but normally producers appreciate the help."

Yes, all rules have exceptions, so feel producers out and always respect their wishes. "We did a makeover segment for *Today* that showed women who wear uniforms to work how to express their individuality on the weekend. I found one of the participants (who was my client) but the producer put it together."

Book It

We happen to think book and author pitching needs the most help. It is the area where the most TV bookings are lost. Around 150,000 to 175,000 new books are published each year in the United States, and their pitches all look exactly the same, right down to the paper they are printed on. It makes us crazy! There are so many books that have the potential to make great TV segments. A book should be an easy booking but it's not, and at the root of the problem is the pitch. It's almost as if the publicists have one letter they all use, and they simply change the title of the book and the author's name. The press releases are neither personal nor relatable, and they are very rarely visual. They are never geared toward a specific show; they are mass mailings. With that kind of pitch your book doesn't stand a chance, unless it's Paula Deen's new cookbook or a high-profile celebrity autobiography or tell-all.

Here's the truth: when we get books we usually throw them into a pile (the press release, unread, still in them), which we affectionately call the Book Wasteland. We wish we could show you a picture of the *bins and bins and bins* of books that end up in the free pile (what we call swag) at TV shows. Other producers tell the same story. If you don't have the time to sit down and write a personal, tailored letter to every show producer, what makes you think we are going to give you the time of day? We do not have time to read press releases and figure out segments from them. Let's go back to what we said earlier: producers need to fill segments. If a new title comes in with a specific segment idea based on the book or author, a booking is practically a done deal.

The publicist may tell you it is not cost-effective for them to send out individual letters and that it makes more sense to do a mass mailing "to see what sticks to the wall."

If your publicist is not going the extra mile by sending out custom pitches, take matters into your own hands. Just let the publicist know what you are doing—most won't object as long as they know what you are up to. If they do, find another publicist. I can tell you we are more prone to book authors if they have taken the time to pitch us personally. We do not care if it is coming from a publicist at a big publishing company. It makes absolutely no difference to us at all, nor to any producer we know.

"One of the things you want as a publicist is for the author to share ideas with you, since they know their subject better than anyone," says Cindy Ratzlaff, vice president of brand marketing for Rodale, Inc. (publishers of many best sellers, including *The South Beach Diet* franchise). But not all books get equal attention from a publisher, so Cindy recommends establishing an honest relationship with your publicist. "You can check in with a pitch idea and the publicist can say, Yes, I think that is a good idea. I do not have time, but I recommend you do X or contact Y," she says. In this way you can work with your publicist and get his or her advice, but still take charge of your book pitches.

"The greatest ally you can have is your publicity department," says Anne Sellaro, executive producer of best-selling author Nicholas Perricone's television series, and his writing and PR partner. "They open the doors. But you have to follow through. It is important for you as the author to come up with the talking points. If your book has seven chapters, come up with seven segments based on them," she says.

Anne makes a key point: a good book pitch tells a story. The most interesting thing about the book is not necessarily the book. Say the book is about money management, but the really interesting thing is that the author was poor and on welfare at one time. That's interesting. How can you make the information in your book relatable or relevant? Can you attach it to another issue or problem?

Albert Lewitinn, of CNN's *Showbiz Tonight*, says many times all he needs to put on an author is one salable nugget from his or her book. "Don't hide it. If there is any support material other than the book, we'll take that, too. We don't even have to have a tape, a photo is fine," he says. "If you were a business branding expert and wrote a book about it, you could tie in to a news story about Jessica Simpson changing her hair color to brown or red. She is protecting her $40 million brand—so you could have an angle on the brand and business of Jessica Simpson. That's a nugget of info that would get you on TV," he says.

Most authors need media training as well. Just because you wrote a book—even a great book—does not mean you will be great on TV. If you get a huge booking like *GMA,* be aware of what someone like Diane Sawyer is looking for. "You need to talk in ordinary terms and not make it a speech. What happens in many cases is that the guest gets coached, particularly book people, and they sound like they're giving a speech," advises the *GMA* coanchor, who's interviewed her share of writers. "It needs to be a conversation," Diane adds. (See chapter five for details on media training.) If you are not good you will not get asked back. That "tip" goes for any guest, of course, not just authors, but they do seem to have a harder time in front of the camera.

Perfect Products

There are two key points about pitching products. One, always send samples so the producer can see, taste, touch, apply, or use it (and approve it). Just remember that most shows are connected to news organizations and they cannot accept elaborate gifts. Second, do not expect a show to devote an entire segment to your product. Product pitches must be idea pitches that incorporate the product.

"Let's say you make hot chocolate. The pitch can't be 'Let's do a spot on my hot chocolate.' No!" exclaims *GMA*'s Raina Seitel Gittlin. "We can't just do a commercial on your brand. If you have something relevant or newsy about chocolate, such as a study showing it's good for your health, there you go. That is your news peg, that's helpful," she explains. Even then, don't expect the spot to talk about only your chocolate.

"A show is not going to do a segment on David's Bridal," says Charly Rok, who reps the dress retailer. "But they will do a spot on how to dress up for less, and we can use David's Bridal as an example," she says. If you can find a magazine editor or expert to do a segment and include your brand in it, that's even better. "Magazines and newspapers are so important because the editors are often called upon to do roundup segments or trend segments and if they know and like your brand or product, they will include it," says Charly.

Jenn Cohn, a beauty publicist at Alison Brod Public Relations, agrees that product pitching is all about pitching trends and news. "Say you have a product that contains truffles—that's a fact or feature of the product. Turn it into a trend," she says. Find a restaurant that serves truffle ice cream, a celebrity who says they love truffles." That's a segment: Mad about truffles! We love Jenn's Sweat Chic pitch—she had the challenge of promoting a deodorant. "It was August and I thought, Everyone is so hot and sticky, let's do a 'make sweat glamorous' pitch. I rounded up five or six other high-end antiperspirants and pitched the idea to the *Today* show. Ann Curry interviewed me and it was great—humorous but informative," she says.

It's Your Turn

Here's an assignment: Don't go any further in the chapter and answer these questions:

1. What is your idea?
2. Why is the idea or pitch relevant? Is the person at home

watching the show going to learn something new or useful? What's the benefit?

3. Who are you? (What's your story? Why are you qualified? See the bio you wrote in chapter two.) Where does your credibility come from? Did you write a book or magazine article? Do you own a business? Did you experience something firsthand? Did you create a product out of a personal need?

4. How is the pitch expressed visually?

Next, distill the answers into a one-line active description and three sentences or bullet points. List three to five possible visuals. You want to end up with a pitch that is a genuine segment idea, from start to finish. If you can't do it in the first round of writing, put the pitch away for a day and come back to it later. Keep working until it's concise, tight, and exciting. That's your pitch.

How to Talk to a Producer 101

Say you pitch a producer and they call you—or you're asked to call them! If that happens, and they are on the line, respect their schedules. Don't waste "airtime" with empty statements and long explanations. **You have fifteen seconds before they get distracted and stop listening, so be clear and direct and fabulous: who, what, where, when, and why.** If you can, site a relevant trend or recent statistic to make your pitch sound newsworthy.

Write out your pitch before you call (see the assignment above) and have it in front of you to use as a cheat sheet. Even powerhouse publicist Cindi Berger says she has her bullet points in front of her before she calls a producer. Don't call unless you feel confident, well rested, and enthusiastic about your idea. If you are not excited, why should we be? You need to believe in your own segment and convey that the show would be lucky to get it without coming off like an ingrate or as arrogant.

If possible, drop a name or make a connection. "So and so says you're terrific." TV people have big egos—flatter them and make sure they know you watch and like their show (see chapter three), as in, "Oh, that dream wedding series was amazing." Or "The piece you did on the president's tax cuts was really provocative."

Do not leave open-ended conversations. You want to close the deal by the end of the phone call if you can. Ask, Can you let me know if it is a yes or a no? The producer probably won't give you a definitive answer, but do the best you can. If the conversation went well, you can at least ask them if you can follow up with them in a week or so. Try to get their direct number or e-mail address, so you do not get lost in the phone tree or spam folder.

There is a line between persistent and annoying, and once you have crossed it you get labeled as high maintenance. At that point the producer is done with you forever. "I do not want to be badgered," says Julie Cooper, coordinating producer of *Wife Swap* and a veteran of *The View* and *Extreme Makeover*, echoing the sentiments of every other producer we know.

"There is a rib place that's popular with celebrities and I called and asked their PR company for a tape of the chef," says Fran Brescia, formerly of *Tony Danza* and now at *The Martha Stewart Show*. "I told the publicist that I will work in the chef when I could. I am honest, take my word for it—I always tell people if it is not going to work. But the PR person calls me every three days. There is nothing more frustrating than that. Between her and the cereal guy who won't stop calling, it's crazy. Now I don't want either one on the show. If you call too much, just forget it," Fran explains.

If you get a producer's voice mail and his or her message indicates it is okay to leave a brief pitch and contact info, take heed. "I get inundated with pitches," says Fran. "Short, sweet, and to the point is best. I delete long messages without listening to them because I don't have the time."

Most producers don't object to well-timed and respectful follow-ups. In fact, if done well, the follow-up is a good way to start building a relationship with a producer. "Send a Christmas card or an e-mail once in a while, especially if you have been a guest on the show," suggests Adam Spiegelman, segment producer of *Jimmy Kimmel Live*. "I definitely forget people, so reminding me is not so bad—just don't do it a thousand times in a row."

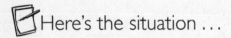 Here's the situation ...

Timing is everything

When I produced **Rosie,** people would call me in the morning—why? That's when our **live** show was on! Use common sense. In general, Fridays are a good time to call because most shows are not taped then; they are "down days." Find out when the show is being taped, and whatever you do, **don't call then.**

Terence

Right in Your Own Backyard

Do not overlook pitching to local media outlets. We've never understood people who say they do not and will not pitch local TV. What a mistake! First, you cannot expect to get booked on *Today, GMA,* or *Oprah* right away. Yes, some people do, but it is rare, even with the help of a manager or fabulous publicity person. Getting a spot on a local show is easier. That's only one reason that most people start out with local appearances. If you have a storefront or a professional who offers services in a particular area of the country, local television is actually going to do more for your business than a national appearance because you are reaching a targeted market of people who can immediately access you or your service or business. "Local pushes the meter up," says publicity executive Charly Rok.

National TV producers are actually quite aware of local personalities—you won't go unnoticed. Some of your favorite hosts started in local TV, including Katie Couric, Oprah, and Rachael Ray. A reel of local appearances gives a national producer an idea of your skills and TV presence. National producers may also feel that they have made a discovery when they find someone from a local market. They welcome reels that contain only local appearances—in fact, both of us have booked and worked with many people who started in local markets. Local appearances give you a chance to hone your on-air skills.

"The best candidates for our talent showcase come from real people," says Adam Spiegelman. "I must get a thousand tapes. It makes my life easier if a person sends me a spot they did on a local show. They can get their shtick down that way."

Chef Deborah Scott, who you met in chapter two, is a firm

believer in local media. "It gives you tremendous recognition. Customers love it when they see you on TV and they very well may think, 'We haven't been to Deborah's in a while, let's go,'" she explains. Deborah says she never advertises because it is so expensive and it has hit or miss results that are hard to measure. "**I always agree to do TV because all it costs is my time, and it is so worth it.**" Not only has local television led to more customers at her restaurants, it has created a new business venture for Deborah at the local level—but it could certainly go national: natural food retail giant Whole Foods is now selling a packaged version of one of Deborah's most famous dishes, a roasted-nut-crusted Brie. "It is available in seven local stores, and Whole Foods promotes it as a local specialty," she says.

Dr. Susan Taylor, a Philadelphia-based dermatologist and the author of *Brown Skin,* a book about skin care for women of color, says local television is essential for her business. "Even if I do not see immediate results, the appearances count. I have new patients months after an appearance, and they say, I saw you on such and such a program—and I cannot even remember which one it was! I also think being on the local news gives me credibility. I have been on *GMA* and the *Today* show and I love that national exposure for my message, but I do not think I have ever gotten a new patient from those appearances. When I do local, I always get a handful of new clients. "

Roundtable: Local Color

Television reporters, hosts, and producers see firsthand the impact local appearances can have. We talked to five of our favorite local reporters, producers, and bookers about the impact local bookings can have on businesses, and what it takes to pitch them. Depending on the kind of local program the on-air reporter is also the writer and producer of his or her segments, as is the case with **Allie McKay** and the local O&O CBS station in Salt Lake City, Utah; **Gina Glickman** of News 12 Long Island, in New York; and **Jill Scott,** of the local twenty-four-hour cable news station NY1 in New York City. Local news or magazine shows may have dedicated talent bookers such as **Jami Osieki,** who books guests for *Ten!*, which airs on a local NBC station in Philadelphia, or senior producers such as **Christina Vandre** of the Gannett-owned Minnesota noontime show *Showcase Minnesota* on KARE-TV.

> **Starring You!:** *All five of you know firsthand how meaningful local exposure is.*
>
> **Gina Glickman (News 12 Long Island): People have no idea how lucrative local television is.** You are reaching your patrons—the people who are going to take advantage of whatever you offer. People who use local TV become well known in their community. There is a planetarium on Long Island and it has been there for fifty years. They were not doing well, and then they came up with the idea of bringing in spinning bikes and offering a "spinning under the stars" class. They did not have dollars to do the advertising. I loved the idea and ran a segment on it, and after that the classes were sold out. National TV cannot do that for you. We connect to where you live and your everyday life.
>
> **Christina Vandre (*Showcase Minnesota*):** When you take advantage of local media you are speaking to an audience who can access you directly. Even celebrities and

national figures benefit. We have heard from theater owners that there is a substantial spike in ticket sales when the star of the film has been on our show. The person seems more authentic when you see them talking to a host of a show that you may see at the grocery store, as opposed to seeing them on a national program.

Jami Osieki (NBC *Ten!* Philadelphia): We book both national and local guests, but what makes us unique for viewers is our local flavor. Viewers hear the same thing from nationally known figures on the national shows. Of course, if Wolfgang Puck wants to come on the show, we welcome him. But we treasure our local talent. We have a local woman who does celebrity gossip, a neighborhood writer who talks about music, and we feature many chefs from area restaurants. Dr. Susan Taylor is the person we go to for skin care—she is the perfect example of a local person who can boost her business. We link to her Web site from ours. A local chef is now appearing on the *Today* show because of his exposure on our show—people watch.

Allie McKay (CBS Morning News, Salt Lake City): As one can imagine, the morning news tends to be a little lighter and more fun than the later "hard news" shows. So it lends itself to more entertaining yet informational features about local businesses and trends in the community. I look for guests who have something to say that appeals to our core audience—mothers and families.

Jill Scott (NY1): Helping bring local businesses and entrepreneurs to the attention of viewers (I cover only the five boroughs of Manhattan, Queens, Brooklyn, the Bronx, and Staten Island) is the most rewarding part of my job. I did a story on a custom handbag designer, Roberto Vascon. He had a crazy story; he came from Brazil and did not speak English. But he did notice that women were obsessed with handbags and so he made some and sold them at a flea market and someone from the *New York Times* bought one and that put him on the map. He had five stores eventually! But then someone swindled him and took all his money, and he was actually homeless for a while. He went back to Brazil, and then came to New York to try again, and started selling his handbags at a local flea market. Again, someone from the media bought a bag and I heard about it, and I did the story. He was really on a financial brink at the time, and he said the day after my story ran he sold an obscene number of bags and made $30,000. It made me feel good because he is a really nice, hardworking guy.

SY: *What about pitches—what do you like to see?*

GG: Something that stands out from the competitors. If it's a nightclub and they do salsa night, what's different about it? Maybe it's the fact that they offer a singles' salsa night. The fact of the matter is most of my segments end up being one or two minutes, so what's going to get someone to look up and watch for that moment? I cannot stress enough how important it is that people be passionate and excited about their idea—that gets me excited. For instance, the owner of Governor's Comedy

Club on Long Island did a four-course date night dinner. There are so many comedy clubs but he put a spin on it and I took it from there.

CV: We are an hour-long live lifestyle show, Monday through Friday. I book six guests a day, from cooks to gardeners to authors to someone talking about a local community event. The topic must be worthwhile to our viewers. We do not want to have people come on to simply chat about a business. It must be news they can use, tips and info they can take away. We like local authors because they often get left out of national pitches. We encourage them to pitch us directly. We never feel anyone is bugging us, and we try to get back to him or her in a timely fashion. Just make sure the pitch is not a commercial. Even though we are sales friendly and do offer sponsored segments, they must contain real information a viewer can use. We do only one or two sponsored segments per show and they are fully disclosed to viewers. It simply means that a company has paid for the segment and their product or service is featured in it, usually with a company spokesperson. It costs about $2,500 for a five-minute segment.

JO: You should customize the pitch. I get maybe twenty-five to forty solid pitches per day. You can weed out the bad from the good very quickly. The ones that are part of a mass e-mail are deleted. The more specific you are, the better. Anything that starts with "Dear Jami" is more prone to get read than one that says "Dear Friend." The idea also has to appeal to our viewers, who are women age twenty-five to fifty-four. If it doesn't but it's still a good idea, we will tweak it to gear it to the viewer. We also look to local authors and local publishers for guest ideas. Locally high-profile people are good. The City Tavern chef comes in and styles his segments as if he were doing the *Today* show. He takes such pride and that's important, too—respect for the local viewer. Passion is half the battle—if you believe in what you are talking about, it is a pleasure to feature you.

AM: I prefer a well-thought-out pitch via e-mail to anything else. An e-mail that includes a brief explanation of the story and how they would go about achieving it visually in the time given, and all the information on how the viewer can get a hold of them is key. We link everything to our station's Web site, so the viewer can log on and find the story (usually a video clip or the transcripts), find the Web site to the shop/author/event, and then contact them directly for more info.

Anyone who calls or e-mails and says, "I have some interest from another station as well" can forget it. Threatening to do a segment on another station isn't the brightest thing to do! I have actually called a place of business that I thought would make a fun and visual live shot, only to be told, "I can't pay my employees to come in early." My segments amount to thousands of dollars of free publicity; they're not something you should pass up. So I called their direct competitor and after the live shot the initial company called and begged to be on the show.

I look for stories that make life a little easier, a more

simple way to do something, or fun places to shop or visit in the community. For example, a chef who can show you alternatives to the same boring school lunches . . . or the latest in maternity wear at a boutique that focuses on hipper fashions or summer hair trends. Can you tell, my segments are not brain surgery? Salt Lake City is very kid friendly—any story for a mom on the go will catch the viewers' interest. I live in Park City, once voted the "Best Dog Town" in America. Utahns love their pets almost as much as their kids! So animal stories are great. Due to the bigger families here, any stories on saving money, whether it is at the grocery store, shopping for school clothes, or family vacations, are a huge draw.

JS: I probably get fifty pitches a day and sometimes more. My voice mail makes it very clear not to leave pitches, but to e-mail me. I am a one-person show, writing, producing, and reporting, and very often I'm the cameraperson, too. I cannot call back! If they leave a pitch on the phone anyway, I delete, delete, delete. If you can make a connection in an e-mail like, "Hey, we met here" or "We were together on a shoot" or whatever, that would catch my eye even if I do not remember you. If the e-mail says "Dear Editor" forget it!

I need stories that have value for the viewer. It's not enough that you opened a great new spa. I would be more likely to come if you said everyone's hair is either limp or frizzy in the summer so let's go to this spa and fix the problem. The story has to have a strong visual component. I'll do something as simple as how to buy fish by taking the viewer to Chelsea Market and talking to fish experts there. Or I may do a segment on how to buy the perfect pillow and go off to a bedding store. Sometimes people call and say I have a great author, but books are not visual, so you have to come up with an angle like a related field trip or demonstration.

And be careful when pitching—review your letter before you send it. I once got an e-mail that said, "Dear Jill, I have a great story and I want to give you an exclusive. I have not seen you in a while Tony . . ." I wrote back and said obviously you are offering an "exclusive" to more than one person! Be honest.

Please pitch in advance. I shoot a week ahead in a perfect world but I like to leave a window so if a story bails I can get something else quickly. If it is an evergreen story, it does not matter as much, but for events I need advance notice.

Handling the Big N.O.

If a producer passes on your idea, it does not necessarily mean it was a bad one. Producers pass on well-thought-out, targeted ideas for a million reasons—they have something similar lined up (that you could not possibly know about), they don't need more segments at the moment, or they are just busy and it's easier to pass right now and think about it down the line. Or maybe he or she is in a bad mood and your pitch is the unfortunate recipient of the gloom. It happens.

"Don't get discouraged if I say I don't have any room for your pitch right now," says Julie Cooper. "Honestly, I will be sitting in my office three or six months down the road and look at the pitch and think, I can include this person now," she says. We could not agree more. Remember that producers move around from job to job. They take their Rolodexes and databases with them wherever they go, so while you may not work at one show you could work at their next show. And they are always calling one another, so your name might get passed along to another producer. We met with an event planner and we had nothing for him at the moment, but not more than an hour after he left our office I got an e-mail from Julie Cooper asking me if I knew a great event planner in LA. This guy was in LA. So I connected them. It sounds improbable, but it happens all the time.

Terence recently met with an on-air talent and was not impressed with her in the meeting. He thought he had heard the last of her, but she followed up with a note that was very focused and made him want to give her a second look. Remember, the producer or booker might be having an off day. Maybe she was great and he could not see it that day. The point is, don't give up after only one try and *always* follow up after any conversation, e-mail, or meeting. It makes a difference. Pitches are like seeds—you are planting them in the minds of producers. Sometimes they sprout right away, and sometimes it takes a while for them to germinate.

On the other hand, there are times when we get annoyed. Terence was searching for a relationship expert, and this one fellow sent him a tape. He called Terence every day and sent him e-mails continuously. He was a pest—very annoying. That kind of behavior signals to a producer that you are high maintenance (HM). We'll work with HMs if they are famous or really good at what they do, but for you, the yet to be discovered, being an HM is the kiss of death. Sometimes people ask us if they are being annoying, and we are always honest. Producers who do not have our experience will lie to be nice, though, so don't always count on their honesty. If someone tells you that you're being overbearing, do not be insulted. Look at it as a huge favor, because if you have a brand your behavior might be hurting it.

So when do you know it's time to give up and try a new tack? "You have to be able to take a hint," says Raina Seitel Gittlin. "If you have reached out to the producer by calling her three times with no response, don't call again," she says. It's not that we are rude, but we do get busy and sometimes we just cannot respond to every call or e-mail, especially if it is something we are not interested in. As Raina puts it, "Gauge your audience and know when to quit." As Marta likes to say, when one door closes, another one often opens. If you get a no, just pick yourself up and try some other way. Move on to the next show and producer.

The sound of silence can be deafening. When author, style expert, and former Style Network producer Elycia Rubin was promoting her book, *Frumpy to Foxy in 15 Minutes Flat,* she would pitch and e-mail producers and never hear anything, let alone a no. "It's surprising, because I have spent fifteen years working in television myself, so I know how to pitch. And I thought professional courtesy would at least result in a phone call saying yes or no." So what do you do when your queries go unnoticed? "Move on to the next person. Just keep going. Somewhere down the line you'll connect with someone who does have a few seconds to respond," says Elycia. That persistence has paid off in bookings on the *Today* show, *The View*, and numerous other national and local television shows.

Tape Measure

Before you go any further—make sure you have a tape of your-self ready to go; *most* producers want to see if you're good on camera before they book you. "I don't mind if it is a home-made tape shot in their kitchen," says Fran Brescia, "but it should be current." She tells the story of a very well-known food storage container company that wanted its spokesperson on a show she was producing. "It was an old tape—and they had no press kit either. There is no excuse with all the readily available technology today," she says. "I told them to go into their warehouse and shoot something new!"

On another occasion, Fran asked a chef for a tape. "He sent me a 1998 *Today* show appearance. You could tell how old it was by looking at Katie Couric's hairstyle. That does not help me. Better to say you have appeared on the *Today* show and send a tape you made in your backyard yesterday," she advises. Remember, you do not want to look like you've been around since radio was new; the goal is to appear fresh. Terence has booked people who are TV veterans but their reels had "new-ness" about them—there was no footage from shows that went off the air five years ago.

Adam Spiegelman books a lot of "real people" talent seg-ments on Jimmy Kimmel, like the guy who eats ten thousand Big Macs in a year, or the elderly woman who collects potato chips shaped like famous people (America really *does* have talent!), and in those cases tapes are essential to make sure potential guests are not too weird or over the top. "So many times they don't have a tape, and it's frustrating." Everyone has or can beg or borrow a video camera. "That's all I need. Something simple that gives me an idea of your personality," says Adam.

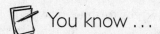 You know ...

Creating a current, appealing tape is "reel simple"

I can't tell you how many people I know who want an on-air career and don't bother taping themselves—or asking the producer for a tape—when they are on a show. So if you do get booked, make sure you make a tape.

- Do shoot your own inexpensive tape if you don't have any TV appearances under your belt.

- Do add local appearances to your tape.

- Do choose your best moments when you are talking or demonstrating.

- Do remove dated appearances (anything more than three years old has to go; old clips actually hurt you).

- Don't put entire segments on—producers don't have time. Five minutes tops is fine.

- Don't add a lot of fancy screen gymnastics, such as wipes, fades, and background music.

- Don't cover your voice with music—we want to hear you speak.

- Remember: producers want to see what you look like, how you sound, and what you project from the screen.

Terence

That was some lesson, wasn't it? Getting interest for your pitch has to do with how good your pitch is, of course, but it also has to do with the luck of the draw—so you have to constantly be out there feeding producers new ideas. Pitching isn't even the half of it—you have got to shine when you get on air, and then develop a strategy that keeps you there. Take a deep breath—the camera is about to be turned on you.

 ## It's a Wrap

- Make sure your pitch is specific to the show.
- Don't call in a pitch when the show is taping.
- If you say your pitch is "exclusive" make sure it is—don't send it all over town.
- Create a tape or "reel" that shows you as you look today, not ten or even five years ago.
- Don't get discouraged if you get a "no"—keep trying.

Chapter 5

The Welcome Guest

Your first, second, or third appearance on TV is the beginning of what can be an enjoyable and beneficial relationship with the media. Prepare, do your homework, and you will deliver an effective message that furthers your goals—and increases your chances of getting asked back or scoring additional appearances on other shows and networks. **A single appearance is not your only chance to make good, but it's important that you treat every appearance with the attitude that it's a Hollywood premiere—all eyes are on you!**

You are seducing viewers with your persona, delivery, and demeanor. There are five keys to being a spirited, and effective, TV guest:

1. Dress the part.
2. Come prepared, have a plan, and plan for the unexpected.
3. Ramp up your ENERGY.
4. Own the interview/meeting.

5. Don't be high maintenance—no divas allowed!

Mastering these five items has rewards beyond having a terrific TV experience—they help you become more appealing professionally and personally. In short, they're the basic ingredients required to be a successful person.

Look Here!

TV is a visual medium. Your appearance is of primary importance. Ultimately you are the spokesperson for yourself, and how you look is one of your most powerful (and memorable) calling cards. It helps establish the image you want to project. And producers *love* it when guests show up looking appropriate and put together. It may take a while to get on TV—start your personal transformation *now,* when you have the time to perfect your look. It's a process to lose weight, get in shape, whiten your teeth, and find the right makeup, hairstyle, or wardrobe.

Talk to the producer about any wardrobe protocols. Take into account the kind of show you'll be on and the time of day it's shown. You might pare down your look for a morning show and get a bit more dressed up for an afternoon show such as *Oprah*. If you were making an appearance on a late night variety show, such as *The Tonight Show* or the *Late Show with David Letterman,* you could go a bit glitzy. However, if you're booked on a serious news show, business formal is the way to go. You can be more casual on a daytime lifestyle or relationship show such as *Tyra Banks*.

Your façade is part of your brand and message: Look like who you are and what you stand for. Have your "television look" established before you get the producer's call, so you are ready to go when it happens. Go back to your assignment from chapter two, when you wrote your biography (see how important that project has turned out to be). It gives you a place to start in terms of how you should look whenever you make any kind of media appearance. What kind of wardrobe and style will instantly give viewers a clue to your expertise, personality, and profession?

Appropriateness is paramount. One woman we know of, a professional home-safety expert and problem-solver, is famous among producers for the wrong reason. Her TV outfit consists of skin-tight jeans, inappropriate revealingly low-cut sweaters, and super-high platform shoes. Her hair is never without a pouf and bleach job. As a result, none of us buy her expertise (nor do viewers), and we would hesitate to take advice about how to survive in a crisis from her. She looks like a pole dancer who would squeal in horror at the site of a mouse. "We like her energy, but she refuses to change her look, which is totally inappropriate for morning TV and to her message," say *two* different producers at separate top rated A.M. shows. What would producers prefer to see on such a person? That's easy: less obvious and better-fitting jeans, a much more demur top, and practical but stylish shoes. It would also help if her hair and makeup were less Las Vegas–looking and more girl-next-door basic.

A recognizable, consistent, neat, and subtle look helps create a coherent message. Retail and design company Shabby Chic founder Rachel Ashwell intentionally cultivates a certain appearance—fresh white T-shirts or pastel cashmere sweaters, vintage jeans, and gently worn cowboy boots. Rachel never strays from her casual, stylish, "modern vintage" outfit because it's consistent with her brand, which represents the same thing: easy, chic yet nostalgic elegance. If you are a designer, how can you create a wardrobe that echoes the look of your design? What's your signature? A vintage scarf or whimsical ascot? Maybe you always wear an amazing antique brooch or brightly colored shirt with a conservative suit. Caution: whatever your accent or identifying piece is, don't overdo it. **Nothing should detract or distract from what you are saying.**

If you are a gardener, don't show up for a demonstration segment dressed in high heels, a fancy dress, and long red nails. As viewers, how can we trust you to give us good advice about planting flowers or designing a landscape if you look like you are going out for a night on the town? Better to develop an outfit that says "plant expert" clearly—perhaps a crisp white shirt and khaki pants or skirt, with either boots or clogs. If you're a chef, don't show up in formal wear.

One of our pet peeves is when a chef tells us, "I don't wear an apron." Huh? If you're a chef, wear an apron or a chef's coat. If you are a doctor, look like one. One thing we love about Dr. Marc Lowenberg is that he always wears a medical jacket. He looks official, and that makes us want to listen to him. By the same token, if you are a golfer, wear a golf shirt or blazer with your logo emblazoned on it. Whatever your "uniform" is, it can look chic and pretty or stylish and handsome if its components are beautifully cut, well made, cared for, and neat. No matter what, the most important thing is that you feel good about yourself in whatever you are wearing.

It's especially important for "talking head" experts (people who discuss issues, without demonstrations or visual aids) to dress in a way that does not distract viewers from what is coming out of their mouths. "If you are an expert, look like one," says Bradly Bessey, co–executive producer of *Entertainment*

Tonight. "I have a problem with editors from magazines who show up to talk about an issue or celebrity in the news and do not look credible. Many of them are young so they should make more of an effort to look authoritative in the way they dress," he says.

Instead of showing up in office casual, Bradly recommends that entertainment experts fall back on more traditional clothing, such as a simple dress or a suit with clean lines (no weird lapels). Legal, scientific, financial, and other "serious issues" experts should dress fairly conservatively, to establish trust with viewers (and producers). Obviously, there are some exceptions, such as the famous Texas lawyer who wears cowboy hats and fringed shirts. But such anomalies are few and far between, and most people can't carry it off unless it truly is part of their long-standing persona and appearance.

On-air spokesperson for *Star* magazine Tara Kraft says her solution is a basic look that suits her personality but is still professional and authoritative. "I wear dresses because they look neat. Even though I comment a lot on fashion trends I want to be relatable to the viewer at home. Solid colors are great, loud patterns are out. I may wear a pair of the latest earrings or a cool new bracelet, but those items are kept to a minimum. I have met producers who are fashionistas and noticed that even they don't rebook people who are dressed in too many trends or appear too fashion forward. That is a look that doesn't appeal to the audience," she says.

It is very likely that the person interviewing you is going to be wearing a suit. Always bring a backup outfit with you to the studio in case there is a "matching" problem. The person interviewing you, if he is a man, does not want you to look like his twin. This upsets the host (a real no-no) because he wants to be differentiated from you. If a woman interviews you (the producer will tell you who is interviewing you well beforehand), you needn't worry as much about matching her suit. Do make sure, guys, that when you sit down, to pull down and smooth your pants in front.

 I have to tell you ...

White does not work!

Don't wear white clothes on TV. Most experts say that it washes out your complexion and creates bright or hot spots on the screen.

Marta

It has happened that the female host wears a navy pantsuit and peach shirt, and her male guest shows up wearing the same thing, essentially. So it is still a good idea to come with "second helpings." The producer and/or the wardrobe person can help you decide what works best. If you do wear a suit, keep in mind that the camera hates stripes. Patterns such as herringbone or ribbing causes the camera image to zigzag, causing "TV moiré." Light blue, lavender, yellow, and even darker royal blue shirts look good with navy or charcoal gray suits. "And I never want to see bare arms on anyone," says producer Julie Cooper.

Do not forget about your shoes. You want the "last hurrah" to be as neat, professional, and polished as possible—not down at the heels. Don't be lulled into the false sense of security that you will be seen on TV only from the waist up. Often, the camera will show both close-up and full-body shots, even if the interview is being conducted sitting down. One relationship author expert we know about appeared on *Weekend Today*. She assumed that no one would see her from the waist down, since it was a seated interview, so her outfit stopped there. She wore a gorgeous designer jacket. Her hair and makeup were all perfect. With it she wore a long black cotton "broomstick" skirt, black sheer hose (with a few pulls), and black lace-up sneakers! Of course, there were two full shots during the segment and, of course, they were disastrous for her image.

If you are wearing a skirt, super-sheer nude stockings or black tights are good choices, depending on the season. If it's summertime and you want to wear a skirt and your legs are in shape, use a spray tan to give them some color. Sally Hansen makes an inexpensive version that happens to be very good. Don't experiment with it right before a booking—try it out a few days or, if possible, a week before.

 Here's the situation . . .

It's a commonly known fact that the small screen adds ten pounds

It happens. Get yourself in shape. That's good for you as a person, but it also helps with the television aspect of your career. That doesn't mean that model or movie-star perfection is a prerequisite. Far from it: you want to look your personal best. Think of it as Super You.

Terence

Best Face Forward

Look at TV professionals: whether they are tall or short, fat or skinny, dark or light, all of them are well groomed from head to toe. Yes, they have wardrobe, hair, and makeup people helping them. Still, even megastars have issues. "I have bad hair days," says Diane Sawyer. "I just come in to work a little early," and get it fixed. Yet you can learn so much about how to groom yourself from checking out the pros.

Please don't show up for an appearance as a "blank canvas" and expect a makeover. The hair or makeup person will fool with your hair at the studio, but we recommend arriving at the studio with your hair already done. Wear the makeup you normally would, blow out your hair, bring your favorite cosmetics, and let the staff give you some extra TV oomph.

Men have it a bit easier than women, because their grooming choices are more limited. Yet guys still have to be very conscious of how they look. For example, men's hair, no matter the length, needs to look neat and modern without being distracting. Make sure your hairstyle fits your expertise. Terence once booked a hairstylist for a makeover segment called "Hair Crimes," which busted people for having bad hair and then gave them new 'dos. The problem was, *his* hair looked like a felony! He was told to either fix it or forget it—he fixed it.

Men with gray hair should go to the best stylist in town and ask for recommendations for adding some color. We're not talking about going from gray to black, but toning down silvery hair with some darker "low lights" brightens your face and gives you a younger appearance. Don't make any such major changes the night before a show! If you are booked on short notice, get a trim if you have time, but don't try something radically different. Try a new haircut or color when you have a couple of weeks to live with it, "tweak" it, and get accustomed to the change so you feel comfortable.

 I have to tell you ...

Have your hair blown out professionally before an appearance

If you have time, it's a good idea to have your hair professionally blow-dried and styled. This doesn't mean get a new hairstyle, unless you need one, of course—it does mean having your hair styled in a sleek, clean, up-to-date way for a polished, perfect look.

Marta

Women's gray hair should usually be covered, unless your "silver streak" is an integral part of your message (maybe you want to come off as "dignified" or "grandmotherly" and gray hair helps put those ideas forward). No roots allowed! Get them touched up a day or two before you're booked. If you get called for a last-minute gig, use a fast-acting over-the-counter product to blend in roots with your hair color in a matter of minutes. Nice 'n Easy makes a ten-minute product, Root Touch-Up, that's effective in a pinch.

Hairstyles should be contemporary but never overdone (big hair is a no-no). Make sure it's not falling in your face. On the other hand, you certainly don't need "red-carpet hair" for a TV segment; it should be professional and simple. Work with a hair stylist and a colorist you know and trust or who have been well recommended to make sure cut and color is the best and most flattering it can be. Learn how to blow out your own hair properly or try to have it professionally done beforehand.

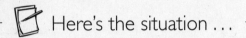 Here's the situation . . .

A bright smile starts with white teeth

Consider at-home or professional teeth-whitening solutions, or even veneers if your teeth are badly stained or yellow. White teeth give you a younger, fresher look—and also give you the self-assurance to smile and speak with certainty.

Terence

Don't forget about your eyebrows—have them waxed, shaped, and trimmed, especially if you have the dreaded mono-brow. If you wear glasses, they should not be from the year of the floods. They must be up to date and suit your face. Eyeglasses have to fit your persona as well. If you are an artist or a musician you can be a bit more avant-garde, but most people look best in simple and modern frames. And please, if possible, do not wear tinted lenses. They are dated, unflattering, aging, and they obscure your eyes. You connect to viewers with your eyes; you don't want to hide them.

Most women know that makeup is an essential part of any public appearance. TV lights are harsh and bright—without makeup you will look pale and washed out. *The New York Post*'s "Page Six" gossip maven Paula Froelich knows first-hand about the power of makeup. When she first made the transition from print reporter to on-air correspondent on *The Insider,* her makeup did not always show off her true beauty.

"It was odd for me in the beginning because I did not know what to do, and no one gave me feedback about my hair or makeup, and I looked hideous," she says. "Never underestimate what the power of hair and makeup can do for you on air. I worship the hair and makeup people at *The Insider.* We used to have crazy people. I ended up looking like Mickey Mouse. One girl would spend an hour on my face and I looked like a hideous, cracked out version of Zsa Zsa Gabor!" she says. "Now we have pros."

 I have to tell you ...

You don't need a lot of money to get your TV look together

Short on cash? Every city has a beauty academy and most offer training sessions with pros working toward their licenses. You can get a blow-dry, cut, or color for free or a small fee. Take advantage of makeup experts at beauty counters at major department stores; they are usually thrilled to give you a new "face" for free—especially if you tell them you are going to be on TV. And personal shoppers at boutiques and larger stores are happy to help you put together a great outfit because helping you is their creative outlet; so don't be shy.

Marta

Guys, you have to be prepared to wear makeup as well. Don't worry—you won't *look* like you are wearing makeup to the viewers at home. Without it, you'll look sallow and older. Invest in a tube or bottle of foundation especially made for men. Studio5ive and M.A.C. both make products men can use for on-air appearances—and both are easily and discreetly available online if you feel iffy about walking up to a makeup counter. Your routine can be as simple as some pancake makeup to even out skin tone and a little bronzer to bring some life and color to your face.

Women need more color on their faces, and it needs to reflect the season and their coloring. "You almost have to err on the side of more is better when it comes to color on your face and cheeks," says *Star*'s Tara Kraft. "The lights wash you out, so you need a great foundation." However, heavy eye makeup should be avoided. For example, choose brown eyeliner instead of black.

If you are going to appear on a smaller national or local show, you may not get a lot of attention from the one makeup person available, so plan on doing makeup on your own. You need six basic items: under-eye concealer, which can be applied on the eyelid as well to hold eye shadow in place; a foundation that matches your skin tone; a neutral eye shadow; eyeliner, if your eyes are not too small; a bright but still flattering shade of lipstick; and a natural-looking blush. Lip gloss is okay on TV as long as it's not too sticky looking. Go easy on super-shiny brands—they look dated and are distracting.

Julie Clevering, a TV makeup veteran (check out her phenomenal work on the Food Network beauties Giada De Laurentiis and Paula Deen), recommends a simple routine that bumps up your normal routine for a natural look. "The proper foundation is important. Get professional guidance to choose the right shade, and in summer, when you have a bit more color naturally, move one shade up in deepness," she says. "And blend, blend, blend," she advises.

"Some people don't blend foundation into their jawline and you end up looking like you are wearing a mask. When I work with Paula or Giada, for example, I look at them from their chests up, not just their faces." Julie also says pink blush adds a pop of color and gives skin a healthy glow. "Make sure eye shadow is blended and your lip color is one you feel comfortable wearing. Avoid outlining your mouth with a lip pencil. It looks harsh and old-fashioned," she says.

Ladies, pay special attention to your lashes. They can help open up your eyes, making you appear awake and alert (especially important for those 5 A.M. segments). Use only waterproof mascara; the standard version has a tendency to run. Better yet, use an eyelash curler: shu uemura makes the best curler in the world (and we do *not* work for them). It costs about $18. Curl lashes once, then put on one coat of mascara and wait a couple of minutes for it to dry, then curl again. Add one more coat of mascara. If you have time and can afford it, consider having individual eyelashes or eyelash extensions applied. It's expensive (from $100 to $300), but worth it if done by a pro. Fake lashes last a few days and lash extensions last two to three months. Makeup pro Julie Clevering cautions women to ask what kind of lash glue the makeup pro uses. Avoid the stuff from China, which she says can take your real eyelashes off when the fake ones are removed.

Nails are *so* important. People do not realize how much they talk with their hands. If you are a guy, we recommend having a manicurist push back your cuticles, because once you cut them you have to keep doing it. No polish! Have them buffed if you want to do something special. Your feet are not going to show, but have a basic pedicure done four times a year. It makes you feel good and that confidence translates to the TV screen. General good grooming adds to your overall positive self-image.

Women's nails should be short, rounded, and polished in clear or neutral. Bright red or odd colors such as purple or blue are dated and not flattering. French manicures are very eighties.

Starring You on Short Notice

Sometimes guests or segments fall through at the last minute and a producer has to scramble to find someone to fill in. If you are a great guest it's very possible that the producer will think of you as someone who could fill in for a no-show. Never pass up a last-minute TV opportunity because you don't think you have time to look good. You do. Elycia Rubin and Rita Mauceri, coauthors of *Frumpy to Foxy in 15 Minutes Flat*, say you can get your look together quickly when a producer calls. And remember, there will be a hair and makeup person in the studio to help finish your last-minute look.

Elycia says women should always have the "foxy five" in their purses at all times. "They will carry you through any occasion, even a TV appearance," says Elycia, who is also a television producer. They are

1. Cover-up stick
2. Pressed powder to even skin tone and eliminate shine (shine is bad on TV)

3. Mascara—it's the one item that does the most for your eyes
4. Blush—for all-over color and a touch of freshness. You can even brush it over your eyelids for a little color
5. Lipstick or gloss

Next, if you get called when you are on the street and you're wearing workout clothes, explain the situation and ask the producer what they have in the wardrobe department. They always have something available for men and women. If you are wearing something really simple and need to jazz it up for TV, women can duck into Forever 21 or a department store for a colorful scarf or some hoop earrings. Men can dash into a department store for a shirt and tie.

Spotlight On: Lloyd Boston

Lloyd Boston, stylist; author of *Before You Put That On*, *Make Over Your Man*, and *Men of Color*; and fashion commentator, knows a thing or two about creating a TV look. Lloyd is a regular style contributor on the *Today* show, Style Network's *The Look for Less*, *The View*, *Oprah*, and We's *Full Frontal Fashion*.

Starring You!: *Lloyd, what are your top tips for anyone when it comes to being on TV?*
Lloyd Boston: The men and women who look great, whether they are professional hosts or seasoned guests, use the power of restraint. That's hard for many first timers, because the urge is to look fancy, and that often means adding clutter in the form of shiny fabrics, pat-

terns, too much jewelry, and elaborate hairstyles. Resist the temptation to add on another accessory—a cool bracelet, a scarf, your granddaughter's angel pin—all of a sudden you're wearing ten accessories. Women and men want to avoid jewelry with movement or noise—it's not a clamor-fest! It's about what you should *not* add on.

SY: *Any other insider tips?*

LB: You should have a bulletproof look that will work for any appearance, ready to go. The clothes you have had in your closet for years that have been through many washings and dry cleanings have a dullness about them that registers as blah on TV. Anchors don't wear on-air clothes outside of work. Take their lead, and have at least two TV-only outfits ready to go. I have an everyday wardrobe and one reserved for TV or live appearances; that way my show shirts and suits always look crisp and pressed and professional.

SY: *What about fit?*

LB: Oversized clothing makes you look big on TV. Too tight in person looks even more so on the small screen, since the camera punctuates your every move and accentuates every feature. Shoot for something that modestly skims the body. I learned that lesson the hard way. Early on in my TV career, I once had too many buttons undone on a fitted shirt. I have very light chest hair but by the time I saw the tape I looked like Austin Powers.

SY: *Specifically, what are some tips for women?*

LB: If you are a woman and will be seated, choose pants. Hosiery can be very tricky on the air. It's a third skin color, which generally clashes with the color of the makeup on your face. If you have great legs and want to wear a skirt, just above the knee or knee length works, and go with bare legs or *very* sheer stockings and flesh or nude-tone shoes with a slim toe and heel for a long, lean look. A black shoe with a heavy heel is very Minnie Mouse.

Fine-gauge cashmere or merino wool knit tops with modest V or crew necks are simple, stately, all-purpose choices. You can wear them untucked for a longer, leaner look when worn over a dark skirt or pants. No novelty sweaters (for example, Santa Claus or Easter eggs).

SY: *What about color?*
LB: In general, color is determined by the mood of the subject you are discussing. If it is a sober topic, choose camel, navy, or chocolate. You can wear happier colors if you're discussing fun or light topics. TV dulls color a shade or two. Obnoxiously bright in person may look just right on TV. The ladies on *The View* sometimes add a pumpkin or other brightly colored sweater because it bounces and brings a certain joy to the appearance of dark clothes, which can be morbid on TV. Drab sophistication in person is deadly on TV.

SY: *Let's talk about the guys again. They should keep it simple, as you said earlier, but it just seems less complicated for men in general. True?*
LB: A suit conjures up a level of respect and stateliness.

If you bring expertise to a segment, a solid-colored navy or charcoal suit is best. It puts you in "the club" because it is a classic design statement. You could wear this suit for all your appearances, even if they are five days in a row, and mix up your shirts and ties. Blue or colored shirts work better than white.

A standard-size lapel with one to three buttons on the closure is best. Pin stripes, excessive shoulder pads, and whimsical handkerchiefs and ties should be left in the closet. Select the finish on the suit fabric carefully. Shiny, iridescent, or sharkskin causes a problem on camera. The general rule of thumb is to unbutton the jacket when seated—just make sure the two sides of the jacket meet, because the viewers may see the unflattering area where the shirt meets the belt. Never, ever button the bottom button—on TV or in life.

SY: *Any final details everyone should think about?*
LB: If you wear glasses, update your frames if necessary and consider getting scratch resistant, nonreflective glasses. LensCrafters offers some good ones—and they are accessible to almost everyone.

Preparation Really *Is* Everything!

Nancy Grace always says preparing for a segment and knowing your stuff is the best way to eliminate fear. Understanding a bit about what is going to happen once you get a booking also sets you at ease.

The routine producers go through with every guest is fairly universal, whether you are on a local or national news or talk show. Knowing what it is beforehand helps set you at ease.

Since your topic is likely based on your pitch, the questions the host asks you are determined well before your appearance. Normally the producer does a preinterview on the phone. He or she asks you lots of questions and they take that information and narrow it down into a script or an outline, depending on the show or what the host likes. An outline consists of bullet points; a script is a series of questions and answers. A briefing takes place at the studio, shortly before you go on air. The producer reviews the script and the questions the host is likely to ask. We've never been fans of sending scripts to people because they end up rehearsing only that and you have to be ready for anything. In our opinion, the best live segments happen when the host does not have to resort to using the script.

CNN's Albert Lewitinn says he always talks to the guests before the show so they are aware they are appearing on a live show. "The microphone is on all the time, so if you want to say something, say it—don't wait for permission," he advises. "By all means jump in there if there is something you have to say. Don't be shy. People talking over each other adds to the excitement."

Producers who film taped segments that follow a narrative (*E! True Hollywood Story,* for example) like to rehearse because they are telling a specific, preplanned story. "I make sure I am personally involved with producing the guest, whether it is in the field or in the studio," says *Extra*'s Rob Sheiffele. "I rehearse them and pose questions until they give succinct answers. Sometimes it takes three or four run-throughs before they get the swing of it. I never feed answers; the guest's knowledge molds the questions. If they flub a line or they are nervous and it's their first time out I put them at ease by saying we can go through the segment as many times as we need to to make them feel confident. We are taped, so we have that luxury," he says.

To ease your anxiety further, make sure you have the right address (yes, it happens that guests go to the wrong place) and show up a little earlier than you've been told. Turning up late is stressful for everyone, and not what you need for your first TV experience. Expect to be greeted at the door by a talent wrangler or a production assistant who brings you to a "green room" area (on big shows you get your own dressing room), where you sit with other guests. Sometimes they separate you but it largely depends on the show and how much studio space they have. Don't be offended if the other guests ignore you—they are lost in their own thoughts, as you should be. This is the place where you get your thoughts together and mentally practice your segment. Respect the other guests on the show—we have not asked people back because they spent the entire backstage time trying to get an autograph. You are there to do your job. Focus.

 I have to tell you . . .

Jumping jacks ease nerves

You want to have energy, but you do not want to be over the top. If you are really nervous and want to bring it down, I often tell people to go into the rest room and do a few jumping jacks before their segment. Sounds crazy but it releases nervous energy and helps establish focus. If you can work out before a segment— which, granted may be difficult if it is an early morning booking— that's even better. Physical activity relaxes and centers you while it energizes you mentally.

Marta

About ten minutes before your segment you will be asked to move closer to the area where you will be seated for the segment. There will most likely be a television set on so you can watch the action. Watch the show you are going to be on, because you may be able to respond to the guest before you, or the host may be talking about you. You do not want to miss that. If possible, ask to see the studio beforehand so you can familiarize yourself with the seating and look of the space. A small thing, but in our experience seeing where the segment takes place makes people feel more comfortable and confident. We would always do that on our shows but don't be disappointed if the producer turns you down for some reason. It may not be possible to bring you to the set before your segment.

And *please* don't come with an entourage. A TV booking is not the time to have a family reunion with the entire clan, even though they may be clamoring to come. That is a producer's nightmare—when they find themselves getting grandma a cup of coffee instead of going over your script.

Come with Your Stuff

If your topic requires a demonstration, props, or visuals, organize what you need beforehand and bring everything you think you need with you. Tell the producer what you plan to bring so they know what to expect. Always bring more than you need—the producer will be thrilled. Most producers appreciate it if you do the shopping and supply everything needed for the segment ahead of time. In short, you need to be self-sufficient and expect very little. When you get assistance, think of it as a gift. Make their lives easier and you are guaranteed to make a great impression.

There are exceptions to this rule, as we discussed earlier. The *Today* show, for example, has union rules and other protocol that necessitates the producer and crew to prepare visuals and demos beforehand, including any shopping that might be necessary for a food or beauty segment. When discussing your segment with your producer, ask them how they like to work and provide them with everything they ask for. Always follow their directions.

A lot of the producers want your props before you arrive so be prepared to supply them at least one day before. If you are an author, make sure the producers get at least two copies of your book and extra book jackets. Chefs bring ingredients, cosmetic surgeons bring before and after photos, and so on. If you are doing a travel segment, have great B-roll ready to go, along with any appropriate still photography and travel gear that is relevant to the topic. Terence can't tell you how many times he has done trip giveaways and travel segments only to find a professional travel company has no B-roll—how is that possible?

Deliver What You Promise

Lifestyle producer Fran Brescia says her biggest pet peeves involve guests who profess to be experts but are clearly not. "One supposed chef came on a show with his PR person and neither of them could decide what recipe to make. It's too bad because he had a great story: he lost weight by reinventing classic soul food recipes to make them lighter. But he clearly did not know how to cook. I helped him for two hours before he went on because he did not even know the recipes that were in his own book. It is either the publisher's or the publicist's job to drill it into them beforehand. It's more work for me, and I will not book them again," she says with finality.

Terence remembers getting a pitch revolving around a cookbook of recipes collected from famous contributors. He booked one of the contributors, a well-known WNBA player, to make "her" recipe for quesadillas. She showed up the morning of a live show with absolutely no idea how to make the recipe, let alone boil water. So there's Terence, who can barely scramble eggs, teaching her how to make quesadillas. He let the host know that the guest did not know how to make the recipe so she was prepared. Thankfully, the host took control of the segment and got through it. That player and everyone involved in the book would never be on the show again. Terence also told his producer friends not to use the book or the contributors or author again.

Another producer describes a fashion expert she booked based on her pitch "Six ways to use clothes to make you look thinner." She showed up with six black dresses. That is not a good segment.

Producers *are* good at fixing things, however, and we know life sometimes intervenes. Just tell us about any issues well ahead of time; we can fix anything. **Do not mislead a producer. Honesty goes a long way in this business.** In the Case of the Quesadillas, the publicist and ball player both said it was the player's recipe. It really wasn't. Maybe she got the recipe from someone in her family and submitted it, but she had never cooked it or felt any connection to it. If you are the publicist, pick the best person to represent your product. Why would you put yourself in that position? Producers are not forgiving when it comes to that kind of stuff.

Energy: Be a Chart Buster

The iconoclastic executive Roger Ailes has remarked (we're paraphrasing) that if he turned down the sound of the TV and he could still tell what the person was talking about that would define a "golden guest." That is why mastering the art of delivery (and talking) is much more difficult than it sounds. People watch TV at home, where there are tons of distractions. Sometimes, especially with morning TV, they are not watching but simply listening as they make coffee or get dressed.

To be golden, you have to reach out with everything you have—your voice, your looks, and your demeanor. All of those qualities can be summed up with one word: *energy*. It's what Marta has always referred to as "finding the light in a person." When she interviews people for the first time to see if they are right for TV, she looks for their sparkle, what aspect of their expertise they are passionate about, and what lights up their eyes. If nothing ignites their spirit, they probably won't do well on TV. Energy is the not-so-secret ingredient that all successful on-air people share. It's verve, enthusiasm, and articulation all rolled up into one fabulous ball. Without it, you're doomed. "If an expert does not give us good energy in a preinterview, we take down their comments and have our talent say it," says E!'s Lee Schneller. Ouch.

Like your outfit conveys a sense of yourself, you want your demeanor to say something about your brand and personality. The political pundit or legal advocate can be fiery and emotional or they may be reasoned and very controlled. Both are good if their delivery has the power to grab your attention. CNN's Albert Lewitinn recalls watching a memorable linguist on a morning show, which proves you can discuss intellectual or scientific topics and still be effective. "She discussed why people use the word *like* so often when they speak. Academics can be very dry, making them tough to work with. But her speaking patterns and delivery was very girl-next-door. If it was anyone else it might have been boring," he says.

"I tell people the segment is going to be the fastest four and a half minutes of their lives," says Albert. "And they always feel like they won't get their point across." Concise, clear, and enthusiasm are the three qualities Albert and all his colleagues like to see in a guest, whether it is live TV or taped. "If you can convey passion for the topic and great personality, you have won the show," he says. How? You can hire a voice coach, but it's probably unnecessary. Practice, dear readers, makes perfect.

Here's an assignment: You have only a few minutes to get your point across, and you want to get to your final tip by the end of the segment. Memorize your five talking points, set a kitchen timer for the length of the segment, and practice answering the questions you reviewed with the producer with a friend. Ask your friend to throw in a few wild-card questions to try to throw you off your game. When stylist David Evangelista started doing TV he would come to Terence's apartment and they would do skits in the living room. Terence would play "host" to David's "guest" over and over until David got it down.

Be conscious of your energy level and *project* it. Be concise and definitive. No quiet talkers allowed. This does not mean that you have to shout (although you may if you get involved in an on-air debate with a host or another guest holding opposing views). Your average energy level translates into dullness on air. TV sucks the life out of you. Sit (or stand) up straight, look at your "host" (your friend) when talking, and try to get to the point where you feel like you are having a lively back and forth conversation while still expressing your views and getting your points across.

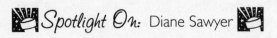

Spotlight On: Diane Sawyer

Does she even need an introduction? Diane currently coanchors ABC's *Good Morning America* and *Primetime Live*. She's a seasoned journalist and even put in a stint working in the White House in the 1970s. She has been a correspondent on CBS's *60 Minutes*. So she *knows* a good guest when she sees one and shares invaluable tips with us. Terence sat next to Diane at a dinner party at director Nora Ephron's house a few years ago. During dinner she talked about a story she was working on to see what he thought—she still advises today that you should try your ideas out on friends and acquaintances. Today we're so fortunate we can share her insights with you.

Starring You!: What makes morning TV unique?

Diane Sawyer: Morning viewers want a conversation; they are having their corn flakes and just want to be part of what's going on between the host and the guest. There is a whole group of viewers in the morning that wants to learn. And, of course, we have a live audience so we get an instant reaction. They are honest and tell us how we are doing, and I always listen to what they say.

SY: So how should guests prepare?

DS: Do your segment with vitality and truth. Talk to viewers like they are smart people, because they are smart and they realize when you are not talking to them, but are just trying to get in your plug. Someone has told them to mention the book or product eight times. Trust your audience and use good instincts.

SY: *What is a great guest?*
DS: When someone is great we don't need to say anything. We all just look up and say WOW! *That* person will be asked back.

SY: *Biggest pet peeves?*
DS: I hate it when someone comes on with a script. I go where I feel, not where the script tells me to go. I always try to stay connected. Don't lie to the viewer. They are much smarter then you think and get very angry when they are lied to.

SY: *What goes into the decision to book a particular guest?*
DS: We have meetings to schedule topics and we are always thinking about what will keep us connected to our viewers. What are they talking about?

SY: *Best advice for those pitching producers?*
DS: Talk to your friends. If they are excited, then mostly likely it is a good topic. I am always asking friends and family what they think of an idea. They're my focus group. I will corner people and tell them about something I am working on. It's not about TV; it's about being real with people. And friends are the best people to practice with.

Own the Interview

Nothing ever goes the way you think it will on TV. Hosts are known to ask their own "unscripted" questions and you should ask the producer whether or not a particular host has a penchant for asking their own questions. It's hard to tell that from watching shows that feature experienced guests who are expert at fielding unexpected queries. At any rate, when a host asks questions that seem like they are out of left field, don't let it deter you from your mission to get *your* points across and *your* agenda met. You may not even want to answer the question the host asks. There are a few classic "pull back" lines experienced guests use to bring the conversation back into their corner. These phrases help you avoid questions you don't want to answer, especially the ones that take you off topic:

"Your point reminds me of what I said earlier …"

"I can't comment on that, but I can say …"

"Your comment brings me back to what I was saying earlier …"

"I see your point, but …"

"Maybe we can talk about that next time, now I want to continue talking about …"

"I'd love to talk about that next time …"

You can also be honest and say, nicely, "I'm not here to discuss that today, what I would like to talk about is . . ."

One producer remembers watching comedian Kathy Griffin in an interview. The reporter asked about her divorce, a subject she had made clear she did not want to discuss. Her retort was very demure and her tone sweet, not combative or defensive: "Now, now, I said I didn't want to talk about that right now . . ." It was very cute and disarming. Watch talk and cable news shows to see how the pros deflect uncomfortable quizzing without getting everyone in the room pissed off.

Star's Tara Kraft gets out of uncomfortable situations by turning reporter's questions to her advantage. "I recently did a satellite media tour with a makeup artist, and we were working with Q-tips. The segment was about how to achieve celebrity bridal beauty. The hosts spent a lot of time trying to get me to talk about celebrity weddings, specifically Ben Affleck and Jennifer Garner's," she says. "I was not there to talk about that, so I simply said, 'I don't know what she is wearing, but I do know she will look great and you can too thanks to our great beauty tips.'" Smart!

Make sure your message is not confused with the interviewer's message. A psychologist specializing in relationships went on the top-rated network morning news show to discuss her first book. This could have been the break she was looking for. A successful appearance on this show could have made her book a best seller and sealed her fate as an important author. When the host said, "So it's true only beautiful women can find mates," she inadvertently agreed with him. This was not her position and, in fact, her book said the exact opposite. She wasn't thinking, and she had not prepared her message. The psychologist called the producer later to see if she could get rebooked with another idea. The answer was no. According to the producer, they got an overwhelming and unfavorable response from female viewers.

Here's another assignment: When you have practiced enough, get out the family video camera (or rent or borrow one), set it up on a tripod, and tape yourself. Watch the results of your mock interview with a critical but objective eye. Use this checklist to make sure you have covered all your bases:

1. Did you look the "interviewer" in the eye?
2. Was your posture good? Did you sit up straight and project?
3. Were you forceful without yelling?
4. Did you communicate your overall message and all of your talking points?
5. Did you field weird questions politely, but firmly, and get back on track?
6. How did you look?

 I have to tell you ...

Practice smiling and talking at the same time

This is a necessary skill if you have your hopes set on being a lifestyle authority. Practice when you are out with friends (if they give you funny looks and ask you, "What's wrong?" you know you're not doing well) or in front of a mirror. Don't push it because you don't want to look like a clown. Also, be sure to have a smile on your face as soon as you are on set because you never know when the camera is going to cut to you.

Marta

Easy Does It

It is so important to be easy to work with. All of the above info helps you become an ideal guest. We cannot stress enough, however, the importance of rolling with the punches and going with the flow. Yes, producers will put up with divas if they are super-famous or the only person on earth who can offer a particular piece of information. Such people are few and far between. The rest of us have to act like human beings if we want to use the power of TV.

People who make it easy, come through on short notice, and are cheerful no matter the circumstances do get asked back and their fabulous reputations spread like wildfire throughout the industry. Terence remembers calling a publicist at a very big corporate PR company when he needed a trip for a guest who was coming on a show. It was 5 P.M. the night before the live program, and the woman said she would make it happen. She did.

The next morning the PR person showed up with the trip and B-roll and was thrilled with the opportunity to share her company's message with the show's studio and at-home audience. After that Terence's relationship was cemented with her, and he would always try to find ways to work her clients into segments. Better yet, she went on to become a big shot at that same PR firm. By making that cruise happen she had a direct link to a hugely successful show. The ability to pick up the phone and get Terence was priceless, and everyone at her company was in awe of her clout. That's huge. Even after ten years she and Terence have a working relationship.

That's the good karma you get from being an easy, reliable guest. It's quite another story when you are difficult. For example, Terence and another producer booked a somewhat well-known lifestyle expert for a segment on a show we both worked on. They arranged for a car to pick up the expert (as is often the case), and unfortunately the car service was all out of standard black limos and sent a white one instead. Well, the expert did not approve and had a fit. He called the show and complained, loudly. Then he sent the limo away and walked.

Terence and his colleague never booked him again and that attitude has prevented the expert from getting other television assignments. The producer who worked with Terence and who is now at another major national talk show recently laughed when a new colleague suggested booking him. "I don't think so" was his reply. Our advice: *get in the white limo*. The White Limo is now our metaphor for all the perceived inconveniences and unexpected occurrences that happen in TV.

Another time Terence was working on a makeover segment with a woman who represents a major hair care line. She thought she could take control by forcing a script on him and tried to cancel certain guests he chose because she did not think they were attractive enough. There is no understanding that the segment has to compromise between product information and what works for the show. Let the hosts say it in their own words; it will be better and more authentic than anything you could write. The makeover subjects also must be relatable to the audience. Terence is not planning on working with that PR person anytime soon.

Don't expect the show to give your business specific billing or plugs. They will try and you should make it available, but it is not always feasible. When you are booked, be clear up front. Say, "I will do the segment and I would like to hold up my book and put my Web address on the chyron." If they can't do it, our advice is do the segment anyway.

Producer Julie Cooper says that while she and her colleagues try to accommodate guests in terms of making sure their product or business is mentioned, they can't always post a Web site on the screen or show an 800 number. "All shows have their own look and policies about displaying information.

It is not the producer's decision whether or not to show a Web address or contact information. Don't harp on it—they will do it if they can," she says.

Get on the Media Train

A media trainer is someone who helps people develop skills to be effective on camera and during interviews. Consider hiring one before your appearance if you feel very unprepared for the camera or right after—you'll have a tape he or she can critique. Your appearance is a valuable tool. We know people who make regular appearances on networks and they still go to training to polish their skills. You're never too good; everyone can always improve, even pros. It's like going to a personal trainer—you don't have to go every day but a refresher once in a while doesn't hurt and can only help. In fact, we're media trainers ourselves but we're still going to work with other media training pros to brush up on our skills before our book tour. Here are some of the things you should learn about a potential trainer:

1. Make sure he or she is the right trainer for your needs. Some media coaches specialize in hosting or in teaching how to read teleprompters or do man-on-the-street interviews. You are looking for someone who specifically teaches how to be interviewed and conduct demonstrations on air. Some specialize in certain expertise areas as well.

2. Ask for references and check them—who has the trainer worked with and what were the results? Be careful. Terence has heard of media trainers who have never worked a day at a TV show. **In our minds the best trainers have at some point been TV producers or bookers. They know what makes a great guest.**

3. Visit their company Web site and read as much as you can about her, including any press she or her firm has received.

4. Ask the trainer to describe the strategy he would use to improve your skills, and what specifically you will learn by spending time with him.

5. Certain media trainers have a particular method they stick to while others (like us) tailor sessions to the individual. We think it is better to go with someone who is not so textbook in his or her approach.

6. Find out what and how the trainer charges before you sign on the dotted line. Some trainers work on an hourly rate and others charge for a package of sessions, usually from four to six. Big city media trainers in Los Angeles and New York are on the higher end of the scale. Trainers in smaller major cities, such as Minneapolis or Boston, may charge less.

Roundtable: Hosts on Great Guests

We gathered a diverse group of the best of the best hosts to share what they think makes a great guest. After all, they're the ones talking to you!

Nancy Grace hosts CNN's *Headline News*'s legal analysis program, as well as a daily trial show on Court TV, *Closing Arguments*.

Paula Deen started her own catering business, The Bag Lady, as a single mom with two boys, and in 1990 opened her own restaurant, The Lady and Sons. She is now the host of her own cooking show (check out our "Spotlight On" interview with Paula in chapter seven), a primte time show (*Paula's Party*), and the author of numerous best-selling cookbooks. Even her sons have a show!

Debbie Matenopoulos was cohost of *The View* from 1997 to 1999 (check out our "Spotlight On" interview with Debbie in chapter six). In 1999, she joined the TV Guide Channel and from there it has been nothing but success. In January 2006, she joined E! Entertainment's coverage of the Golden Globe Awards and quickly became one of the three hosts on E!'s weeknight celebrity gossip and pop culture series, *The Daily 10*. Debbie frequently contributes to VH1 specials, including *I Love the 90s*.

Designer **Isaac Mizrahi** added "host" and "movie star" (if you have not seen *Unzipped,* please rent it right after you finish reading this book) to his résumé after landing his own show, first on Oxygen and now on the Style Network, and designing a highly successful line of clothing and home decor for Target.

Starring You!: *What's your definition of a great expert or "real person" guest (as opposed to a celebrity)?*

Nancy Grace: Passion! Experts who know what they are talking about, and who are connected either intellectually or with the heart of the story I am reporting on. They may be inarticulate or uneducated or not photogenic, I don't care. If they have a compelling, relevant story to tell I want to hear from them.

Paula Deen: The best people are the ones who are themselves—just the real deal.

Debbie Matenopoulos: I want information and I want as much as possible in the two-and-a-half-minute time frame. My goal as a host is to deliver ideas to the audience concisely.

Isaac Mizrahi: Any time an expert has great tips, even if they're off the topic, it's a great segment. Usually an expert with a platform, like a chef who actually runs a restaurant, brings a point of view, as opposed to one who has no practical knowledge.

SY: Any pet peeves?
NG: I hate people who are unprepared; it is a waste of my time and viewers' time. Airtime is expensive. If you are not prepared, do not show up—don't bother. I have one hour to explore the depths of a legal story. And be on time. Guests who always have car trouble—that's a problem. I have gotten out of cabs and *run* to *Larry King Live*. Finally, pundits may not apply. I put on real trial lawyers and reporters who have covered the story. I do not care if they are print or radio—I do not want a "TV shrink." If they come via a PR agency I am suspicious.

PD: People who are not committed. Stick to what you like and be true and honest.

DM: People who talk down to the audience. If the viewers get the feeling that this person thinks they are better than them, you've lost your audience. You want them to feel a part of you and the things you are saying.

IM: Personality, important as that is, can become annoying. When the expert is there simply to promote himself, it's a bore. It's really good when the expert has an agenda and is able to take us through it methodically. It's a delicate balance of charm and information.

Build, Baby, Build

Your booking is the beginning of building relationships with producers that can result in more appearances—and maybe, just maybe, a TV career. It starts with one show. As soon as the segment is over, take some time to thank the producer in person. He or she may be busy with the next segment, but try to make a handshake, eye contact, and a friendly good-bye a priority. **Follow up** *as soon as you get home* **by sending an e-mail or handwritten note thanking the producer for a great opportunity.** In all our years very few people have written us notes, and it makes a world of difference.

Even if you think the segment did not go as well as you think, send a thank-you note or e-mail anyway. That can smooth over a lot of mishaps and mistakes. Then go back to square one. Tape the show and watch it critically to see what you could do better. Take the best parts of the appearance, and start creating your reel. If you can post the highlight on a Web site as streaming video or a download, it's even better.

If you wait more than a few days before sending a note the producer will have moved on and forgotten about you. You do not want that to happen. Since people rarely take the time to be polite, your good manners will make you stand out to the producer, who works thanklessly on most days. Your note should include a few lines that express your hope that he or she liked the segment, and that you have more ideas you will send. Pitch another *great* idea a couple of weeks down the road. If you do get an e-mail back from the producer, ask politely for another lead if the second idea doesn't fly.

Relationship building and creating a platform for your brand or business is not easy, but with time, effort, and patience, it's doable. Once you are an easy guest and deliver, you can have the luxury of calling producers and asking *them* what they are looking for, that is, What kind of segments can I give you? The producers will feel like you are part of their team, working "from the field," thinking about their needs, and bringing them news and exclusives from your area of expertise. Having a relationship like that puts you ahead of everyone else. So let's get moving to the head of the line . . .

 It's a Wrap

- Dress the part—look like who you are and what you do.
- Come prepared, have a plan, and plan for the unexpected.
- Ramp up your *energy* and project your enthusiasm.
- Deliver what you promise—and more.
- Know your topic inside and out so you can own the interview.
- Don't be high maintenance—no divas allowed!
- Follow up an appearance with a thank-you note to the producer.

Chapter 6

Expand Your TV Presence

One TV appearance is great but how do you take that experience and multiply it? What does it take to turn your expertise into a resource well that TV producers want to dip into again and again? There's no magic—it's a three-step process:

1. **Build relationships.** Build and maintain relationships with producers to increase your chances of getting asked back a hundredfold. If you're dependable, easy to work with, and consistently come through with fresh, innovative ideas, producers come to trust you and will use you repeatedly. The low maintenance, gracious, humble guests with usable information succeed. **Don't forget that producers move from show to show—their job jumping is beneficial because if you have a relationship with them they will book you wherever they go.**

2. **Communicate effectively.** Second, producers rebook trusted authorities—you have to know your stuff *and* be good at delivering it. Media training helps (see chapter five) but some people never come across over the airwaves. You have to

be willing to work hard at being good or (and this is hard for many) relinquish your spokesperson role and give it to someone else who can do your brand or business justice. This is particularly important for businesses and the people who run them to know: Just because you are the CEO of your company does not mean you are its best spokesperson—you could be its worst. Nothing creates a bad reputation faster than being a lousy spokesperson. Grooming the right face or faces to rep your brand is critical. Hiring a celebrity spokesperson is an option for some, but beware of pitfalls (negative press or controversy surrounding the person that is unrelated to your brand) in that realm that can hurt your reputation.

3. Develop recognition. One appearance or mention is not going to result in brand or personality recognition. You have to get yourself out there repeatedly, creating as many of what in our business are termed "impressions" with consumers as you can. **Product placement and giveaways are other ways to create brand recognition and to build good relationships.** Getting press coverage is essential, since TV producers get many of their ideas from magazines and newspapers. Booking a satellite media tour is one way of getting multiple hits in a variety of TV markets. Hiring a PR firm is another—but only if they are effective, efficient, and enthusiastic advocates. You need to be their priority, otherwise you are wasting you money.

Relationships 101

In real estate success is defined by the adage "location, location, location." In TV it's all about relationships, relationships, relationships. You wrote a thank-you note to the producer after your first appearance on a show (you did, didn't you?).

Once you've gotten on their radar screen (since few people bother taking the time to show their appreciation, a personal note makes an impression), start pitching them more ideas on a regular basis. Unless you remind a producer of your existence, he or she forgets you in the flurry of new activity.

Here's as assignment: Think like a media strategist. About a month after any appearance, pitch producers with three to four segment ideas that relate to your message, brand, or business *and* something topical or current. Watch the producers' segments to see what they are covering and how, watch the news, and read newspapers and magazines for ideas. For example, you have your own financial services company and the last segment you did was on how to save money for college. You notice that the *New York Times,* the *Wall Street Journal,* and your local news station have all done stories on spa-like retirement communities. Maybe a new spa retirement community has opened in your area. Tell the producer you have spotted a local and national trend (retirement communities) and you can tell people how to save money to afford or invest in these types of communities.

Treat the producer like a confidant by keeping them updated on developments in your area that could be considered newsworthy and segment appropriate. You may get another booking or at least interest for the future. Continue to send the producer a quarterly e-mail with a few good pitches and assurances that you are able to supply them with information or segments about any of their current needs. An occasional handwritten note during the holidays is also appreciated. Another great idea is to offer an editor an exclusive on something; the next time you call they will be more inclined to help you. That's called working the relationship. When you see a not so famous person on a talk show it's usually because there was some kind of trade made. That means a publicist for an A-list star will call a booker on a big talk show and say, I will give you a big actor but in return you have to book so and so, who's starring on a struggling TV show.

Here's another assignment: Network. Producers know other producers (it's a very small world). When a producer passes on a pitch, ask him or her if there are any other producers at their show or other shows who might be interested in the idea. There is a good chance he or she will give you a name (or two)—when you pitch the new contact, mention your producer's name in the subject line. This is the best way to build your contacts and relationships, especially if you are not in the TV business and don't go to a lot of industry events.

You should make every effort to attend events where TV and other media people (including local) might be. You never know where you'll bump into a great new contact. You could meet a contact at a neighborhood block party or at a fundraiser or at your kid's birthday party. Have your business card at the ready and meet whoever you can. Social gatherings are comfortable settings; everyone is relaxed and it's a friendly way to show a potential contact your personality. Don't be overly aggressive (which is a tendency if you are nervous or anxious)—you'll scare people off. But do be confident and reveal your interests when talking to someone you think might be interested in your message.

The best way to maintain a lasting bond with producers, and this is especially crucial for individuals such as authors, experts, and entrepreneurs (who, unlike large companies, are easily replaceable and have very little clout), is to be low maintenance and amenable. We talked about being easygoing in chapter five but it bears repeating here. There is a temptation after you become a popular guest (it's human nature) to believe that the producer needs you more than you need the producer. Wrong. The key concept is *humility*.

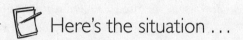 Here's the situation...

You've got to get yourself out there!

The book you are reading now would not have come into being so quickly if it had not been for networking. While we did know a few people in publishing—there is some overlap in the media business, but not a lot—we couldn't call anyone or push a button and say, Hey, publish our book. And, in the beginning, we had only an idea for a book and nowhere to put it, so to speak. Marta went to a book party for friends of hers, Elycia Rubin and Rita Mauceri, who she worked with at E! Entertainment Television, to support their book. Marta met Karen at the party and they talked about the book idea, which Karen thought was a good one. Next, Marta introduced Karen to me and we all hit it off. Karen put us in touch with Claudia Cross, book agent extraordinaire, and the next thing you know, we developed a proposal and Claudia sold it to editor Jeremy Cesarec at HarperCollins. If Karen and Marta had stayed home—well, who knows what would have happened. Absolutely nothing! So get out there.

Terence

Marta learned the virtue of humility while working at E! Entertainment Television. Then president Lee Masters taught Marta and the network's entire E! staff to be confident, yet humble, and never cocky. They worked with top celebrities and movie and TV studios and could have so easily adopted a

cooler-better-hipper-than-thou attitude, but Lee was quick to
nip that tendency in the bud. He sent a personal message down
the ranks to never to be too full of yourself.

Fran Shea, a TV consultant and former president of E!
Entertainment Television, says she used to have a joke about
these X-rays that come out of the camera. "These special 'rays'
would take a lovely, energetic, talented show personality and
with each exposure turn them into a demanding, unreasonable,
arrogant prima donna. It happened so often throughout my
career I came to think the X-rays were real," she says. Don't
let that happen to you, because there is always another lovely,
energetic, talented show personality to take your place.

As head of the talent department at E! for many years,
Marta couldn't help but notice that the talent who were humble and easy to work with got much further along than the
talent who acted highfalutin or who were difficult. That's a
kiss-of-death label unless you are a really big name. If talent,
show guests, executives, or producers for that matter, acted
cocky, E! steered clear. That is not an uncommon scenario in
television, because arrogance and conceit send a signal that
you are HM (high maintenance). In fact, we have actually seen
(and written ourselves) "HM" on TV segment guests' résumés.
Or we have gotten angry calls from the control room saying,
"*Never again.*" We all know what it means: *don't book ever.*

Producers frequently move from show to show, and you want
to go with them. In order to make it into their roving Rolodex (or
BlackBerry or Sidekick) and get into their "rotation" of guests they
count on, you have to be easy *and* willing to deliver the goods, no
matter what the challenges. Be reliable. Follow through, deliver
on promises, and go the extra mile. If we can call you at eight
o'clock at night and ask you to deliver a segment the next morning at 7 A.M., please come through and we'll never forget you.

On the flip side, if you get bumped or canceled at the last minute because of breaking news or an eleventh-hour celebrity booking, please don't throw a fit. Everything changes constantly in TV; expect the unexpected. Accept with grace and we will do everything in our power to reschedule you. Get angry and it's over.

Anne Sellaro helps manage best-selling author and anti-aging authority Dr. Nicholas Perricone, and in that role has

 I have to tell you ...

Create a running database

I started creating a database of contacts before I was out of college and I've never stopped. Now I make my living from it. At that time, I kept a file of index cards, one for the name, title, address, and telephone number of every person I met who could help me land my first job in TV. When I called the contact, I made a note of the date and what I said and what they said. If someone said, "Call me in two months," I would put it on my calendar and follow up. That system is easily transferable to the electronic gadgets we use today. Whenever I interview someone, I take their "vitals" down and enter them into my computer as they speak. I am the brazen one who has the audacity to ask for personal cell phone numbers. When I am looking for a guest, I have no time to call agents and managers; I need the most direct access to the person as possible. This drives the agents and managers crazy but it helps get the person booked faster. Not one person has ever said no to me. I also note what we talked about and include any impressions I have of them. It's very helpful and makes subsequent meetings with these people that much more meaningful and personal.

Marta

proved that building long-term relationships with editors and producers, from the highest to the lowest person, is based on gracious modesty and helpfulness. More than one producer independently points to Dr. Perricone as an "ideal guest" and "in the rotation" because he is so easy to work with.

"Producers always call me up after an appearance and say how nice Dr. Perricone was to work with, how accommodating he is, and he gets rebooked because of that, and because he always delivers useful information in a unique way," she says. His secret? "Just go where the viewers are, never say no to an opportunity, convey your message in an exciting way, and show your enthusiasm and interest to the producers," he says. It doesn't hurt that Anne sends a little product as a thank-you. That goes a long way with a producer—a little exfoliating cream in your in-box does wonders for your mood after a long week of producing guests.

Please do not think that the only person worthy of your good graces is the producer you are working with. Be nice to *everyone,* from the security guard to the receptionist to the intern getting you coffee. They can all help you. Those bright young things you meet at the TV studio—a lot of them are going to be TV producers and executives someday, and they have excellent memories. "I have a good friend who was an intern and now he is a producer of Rachael Ray's new talk show, and we work together—it is *critical* to be kind, courteous, and accountable to *everyone*'" says Jon Harris, vice president of media development and communications for the Sara Lee Corporation. He has relationships with producers today that started as friendships many years ago, before he was at the firm, and when many of them were assistants or even interns at TV stations.

Jon himself started out as an intern at a radio station. When he was just twenty-one years old and working in PR at Bally Total Fitness he was able to book fitness-related segments on that station, including on *The Howard Stern Show,* because of the friendships he made there. And, of course, the publicity he got had a positive effect on the gym. That kind of relationship building has been helpful to Jon's career, which has included stints at Pepsi and now Sara Lee.

Cultivating working relationships with TV producers is *essential* for the success of companies, both small and large. A PR person's job is to get great publicity for his or her company and the only way that's accomplished is by having a rapport with the media. If you are not willing to work with the media and educate them about your brand or message, stories about you will not be fair and balanced—and that's a huge disservice to your company.

"Whatever I can do to provide assistance to a TV producer, whether or not it has a direct relationship to the brand I am representing, I do it," Jon says. That attitude always prevails with producers—but it's one that unfortunately many companies don't have. Jon says he thinks of himself as a resource and for that reason has been able to get his brand booked on many shows, including all the network morning shows. "One year Bally's was able to participate in a 'Fit Today' series on the *Today* show, and that certainly would not have happened if I had not made professional friendships with producers who ended up working there."

Jon recommends that PR or corporate communications professionals (and those of you doing it on your own) make sure that every reporter has their home and cell phone number so the reporters can get in touch with them easily. You do not want to miss out on any opportunity to talk about your brand or message, so make it easy for people to reach you. Being elusive is not going to get you more or better press. "Your job is to be accessible and available. The only way anyone is going to understand your business goals and needs is by telling them," he says. "I have worked with companies that were reactive to only negative stories, not proactive, and it is not as effective."

The other benefit of having great relationships with producers is that everyone can help one another out when necessary. We do things for people as favors *all the time*. When Terence was working on a show, there was a PR person who wanted him to put some children on for a segment related to a kid's brand. He booked the kids even though he knew it might not be a home-run segment. And the host was good with kids and she could make any segment come off well. Terence did it because this PR woman has always come through for him in the past when he needed segment material or products or giveaways. Yes, it's "I'll scratch your back if you scratch mine," but frankly, that's the way our world works. You *want* to build those kinds of back-scratching relationships. We are all giving or repaying favors. If someone does not pay us back we resent it, and he or she is crossed off the list.

When producers *seek you out* for inspiration or to brainstorm concepts and ideas, you know they are your friends for life. Kerri Ross, of Siren Public Relations in New York City, says, "I have gotten to the point where producers call me. Once you establish trust with the media, they will be open and responsive so it becomes a real working relationship."

Lippe Taylor PR wiz Charly Rok says the same thing: "It's so much fun to work out ideas with a producer. If my clients end up in a spot, great, if not, it's still fine because it's part of creating and maintaining an intellectual partnership with shows and producers. In the long run, my ability to get producers on the phone and work with them so closely serves my clients well." Her it's-not-about-me-it's-about-helping-you philosophy pays off: she gets her clients booked on major shows and featured in national magazines and newspapers every month.

Speak for Yourself

A bad reputation comes from being difficult and unreliable, as we've mentioned. But it also comes from being inconsistent with material or delivery. Everyone has an off day; producers understand that. But we have known people who are unpredictably good and bad—and that kind of person gets known for being uneven very quickly. There's a hesitancy to book such a person, even if you are fabulously accommodating and smart.

Unfortunately, some people, including the heads of companies, insist on being the face and voice of their brand and business. Or they assign on-air media relations to the head PR person, who may or may not be good. The idea that just because you're the boss you're good on TV comes under the heading of self-involvement, and it does not serve your business interests well. CEOs may be intelligent but they can be horrible on TV. We cannot tell you how many times this happens, and it can really be a gruesome accident, with spillage all over the TV screen. There is a large casual clothing company that pitched Terence all the time, and he always said no because their spokesperson was the head of PR and she was really boring on TV. How can a major public company with retail outlets all over the world have such a bad media person?

Ask yourself: Am I truly the best person to represent and speak for my brand or company? The best spokesperson might be one of your employees (and not one from the upper management pool—egos can really ruin everything) or possibly an outside hired hand. Get us a *real* person who has innate energy or who can be trained to be an effective expert. If you are hiring a CEO or president and you want that person to talk to the media, make the qualities of a great guest and a good talker part of the requirements for the job. That is a real trend now. In the past, companies might have accidentally hired the right person for TV and for the business. Now more firms have woken up to the fact that TV has the biggest impact on sales and reputation building and they are looking for people who can both run a business and talk about it beautifully.

Joanna Jordan, founder of Central Talent Booking, who books talent for numerous national shows, has a great idea for companies who are looking for the right people to send before

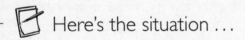 Here's the situation …

Give it away and ask questions later.

I cannot tell you how many times I have called a company for a giveaway and the PR person says no. Excuse me? Those people should be fired on the spot. The answer should be how many do you need and when does it have to be there. Giveaways are incredible exposure for your company and you don't even need a spokesperson for a great giveaway!

Terence

the press. "Hand out an anonymous questionnaire to all your employees and ask them who is the most appealing, attractive, well-spoken, and exciting person in the company. If you give them a chance to be honest, you'll learn something," she says. Joanna attended a dinner party where she sat next to a very deadpan, serious banker type. When he found out what she did he proudly told her he did a lot of TV. "I was on Bloomberg for forty-five minutes," he said. "That must have been riveting!" says Joanna. "You have to be quick, entertaining, and energizing. The last thing you want to do is bore your viewer." Otherwise it's a turnoff, and we mean that literally.

There is another aspect of reputation to consider, and that is enhancing your own or your firm's standing with controlled TV coverage. Segment TV and press coverage is an opportunity to get your side of the story out. There is a misconception some companies (and people) have that if they say nothing to the press, newspapers won't write about them and on-air journalists won't report on them. False. "That's an enormous mistake people make and you are shortchanging your company by not talking to reporters and producers," says Jon Harris. "It has been a very rare occasion that I have met a reporter who wanted to write a negative story about a company I worked for—they do not start out that way," he adds. Stories become negative or at least slanted when companies put up roadblocks.

Jon worked at a Bally Total Fitness and every January a newspaper or TV station would send in hidden cameras to the gym and write horrible stories about it. "I sat down with the CEO of the company and said, Look, you know this happens every year so let's prepare." His advice was to let the media know they are welcome in January and all year round. That way they did not have to worry about hidden cameras and that company made sure the facilities were up to snuff all the time. The company also decided that January was the time to reinforce its corporate and consumer mission with the staff. It worked. "We put these policy changes into place and we went from 50 percent negative coverage to 98 percent positive press in January and all year long," says Jon. The change was immediate and the press began to see the fitness firm as a partner not as an adversary.

Many companies and spokespeople do it right. You meet many of the best in this book. There are a few companies that are creative and effective in terms of spokespeople and that have created excellent reputations with both producers and consumers. That's part of good branding. It's worth taking a look at the following four case studies—even an individual with a great idea can learn something from big business pros.

Beautiful People

Origins is a successful cosmetics company that brands itself by promoting beauty and wellness through good-for-you products and feel-good experiences, and by celebrating the connection between Mother Nature and human nature. Origins is able to create a personal, intimate, almost handmade feeling between its products and consumers, even though it is part of the Estée Lauder Companies, which owns many brands, from Aveda to M.A.C. Origins does this in a variety of ways, but an important aspect of its brand marketing is how the company trains and uses a variety of spokespeople and product tie-ins on TV.

Origins uses internal corporate spokespeople, called guides, to talk about the brand, and brand president Daria Myers and Dr. Andrew Weil, the health and antiaging guru, to talk about the Origins line. "We make sure our internal spokespeople are media trained and filmed so we have a reel of them before we even pitch producers, so producers know who they are getting and that they are good," says Amy Metrick Hornstein, executive director of global communications for Origins Natural Resources. Aside from media training, Origins puts store guides through an intense three-month education on new and reintroduced products so they really know their stuff. Brand president Daria Myers is very eloquent and attractive, so a lot of shows ask for her to talk about wellness and trends. "And, of course, Dr. Weil is always in demand by the media and he's quite practiced with it," says Amy.

Origins recently introduced a men's line of bath and grooming products and had to find a way to talk about it on TV. Amy explains their strategy this way: "We needed an expert spokesman who looks great, but we don't have a man internally who is trained. But we do have great relationships with the magazines. *Men's Health* covered our line, which is a great fit. So we asked the magazine if we could pitch this grooming editor so that he could include Origins in broadcast segments. It's perfect because it's a third-party endorsement, so it comes across much better. We understand the segment is not going to be three minutes on Origins, so we welcome including other brands—we work with what's available. When a producer asks for something they get it immediately."

Often Origins lets the products speak for themselves—a spokesperson is not always necessary. "In fall 2004, we worked with wedding Web site The Knot, who was working with the *Today* show on their wedding series. We provided a spa gift basket that would go along with a destination wedding to Cap Juluca," she explains. It was just one of four in-room gift basket options the audience could vote for.

"We received so much coverage—first they announce it in the tease for the gift basket episode, and showed the basket brimming with products. When the show came on, the hosts talked about all the baskets. I wrote the script for ours, describing what each product does, which the host read. Then they showed it a third time when reminding viewers to vote," explains Amy. The basket was also featured on *Today*'s Web site for a week. Origins' spa basket was not the winning trip, but they were thrilled with the exposure, according to Amy. "We got so much coverage from a single gift basket. If we had won, fulfillment would have been costly, which would have been fine, we would have gladly done it." But "losing" was a win-win situation for the company.

Fit for TV

Bally Total Fitness has a three-level approach to spokespeople. "We have national male and female spokespeople who work as fitness trainers from the clubs. They represent all ethnicities and various age groups and are sent out for segments on national shows," says Matthew Messinger, associate vice president, media development and communications for Bally Total Fitness. The company also pulls from the ranks to suit specific local markets. "If *Good Day New York* or the local Ohio *Today* show wants a fitness person we use someone from a club in those markets who has been media trained," says Matt. Finally, Bally occasionally contracts with outside spokespeople, but they are one-on-one trainers with Bally clients, so they understand the company's brand and fitness philosophy.

"It's essential that we send Bally trainers out as spokespeople. Being on the front lines is critical—our trainers are in the field all the time. They follow the trends and are constantly keeping up with the latest equipment and fitness information," explains Matt. He argues that well-known fitness gurus often seen on TV may have a cachet, but Matt doubts that they are training people day in and day out. "Our spokespeople do it every day. Their demos are useful and consistent."

Because Bally has so many trained, qualified spokespeople all over the country, they can turn on a dime when a media request comes in. "One Friday night I got a call from a producer I knew from a previous show. She was making a pilot and was taping a segment with a couple on that Saturday evening that required a trainer to work with the woman. We had a trainer there the next day and we gave the couple a six-month pass to a nearby facility and a couple of training sessions," says Matt. The fact that he was able to get what the producer needed on short notice adds to Bally's media reputation for agility. "I was there for her and made it work in a short time. That's a good feeling for everyone," says Matt.

It is worth jumping through whatever hoops you need to to get your brand on the air, because it translates into actual business for your company. "We did a media tour for a downloadable fitness e-book we created. The book was accessed through our site, so whenever we talked about it on TV, it drove people to us, and those were leads for memberships, and that translates into dollars," says Matt.

Hospitality Sweet

Kerzner International, a developer and owner of luxury resorts including Atlantis and One&Only, approaches media in three central ways, and none include using specific spokespeople.

Still, the hospitality company conveys its core message, "Blow away the customer," effectively without one. "If you were to look at the budget of hospitality groups, our costs would be far lower than others and our return higher because we use our money in a smart way. We would never send a press release to ten thousand people. We are tactical and careful about presenting our stories," says Lauren Snyder, senior vice president of Kerzner's corporate public relations.

Kerzner has also invested in its media infrastructure to make shooting from exotic island locations easier. There is no easy way to do live segments economically, so the company has begun to lay fiber lines in more than twenty-two locations around one resort that can carry signals to Florida, which are then sent to all of their offices. They can do three live remotes or camera shots at once. All the crew and host have to do is show up with their cameras and do remotes with little cost to them. A weatherperson anywhere in the United States can show the beautiful blue ocean on their screen during a cold and snowy winter. "Our TV visibility is poised to increase enormously once the system is in. I guarantee that technology translates into bookings. As nimble as you can be with what is at your fingertips is a measure of how successful you can be," says Lauren.

Beyond that there are three core strategies the company uses to gain media attention. "First is to bring the media to our destinations. They are breathtaking and therefore visual, so we bring a weatherperson to one of our resorts in the Bahamas, and they say, and can show, how beautiful the beach and the resort is," says Lauren.

The second method is creating entertainment value for shows such as *Entertainment Tonight, Access Hollywood,* and *Extra,* as well as for television stations around the country, by providing B-roll of celebrity events. For example, Lauren says when the stars come out for golf tournaments or charity events or even parties, Kerzner shoots the event and packages it so the entertainment news can use it as part of a story.

The third, and perhaps most effective, method is news creation. Kerzner focuses on what people are talking about or thinking about in terms of travel and resorts and finds a way to address it and package a news story around it. One of the most interesting examples of this is Kerzner's Gentle Travel program, which they developed with Johnson & Johnson. "We have so many families come to us, we service 6,500 cribs a year. We felt that the biggest problem families have is schlepping with all the baby stuff you need and then getting the baby to sleep through the night," says Lauren.

No one has addressed the issue of how to take a vacation with a baby and enjoy it. So the firm approached J&J because they felt their brands were complementary. Before then, the health care product giant had not engaged in the hospitality industry. Together the firms created a kit that includes nighttime creams, head-to-toe wipes, soothing natural washes, lotions, a moisture stick for the baby's face after the sun, a nightlight for ambience, and a lullaby CD. The kit gets delivered in the crib, with an extra set of sheets in case of nighttime accidents. There is only one number you have to push on your phone to get what you need.

"We worked with Jennifer Trachtenberg, J&J's pediatrician, to compile tips on acclimating babies to strange rooms. Our pediatrician-trained babysitters mean families can really make a stay at our resorts an enjoyable trip," she says. They also make baby bathtubs, bottle warmers, and sterilizers available to couples with babies, which are big things to drag with you on vacation. "In this case, we use Jennifer Trachtenberg as the spokesperson. She is a pediatrician who also happens to be the mother of three children," says Lauren.

The Atlantis resort in the Bahamas developed a large marine habitat, which now cares for seventeen Katrina dolphins. "We did live and taped stories and created a B-roll package, which covered everything from the devastation of the hurricane to the loading of the dolphins into specially designed carriers to the animals being reunited and seeing each other," says Lauren. **After the** *Today* **show aired the footage, Kerzner sent the story out on satellite and received more than eight hundred pickups around the country.** "We believe in creating ways to stand out," says Lauren.

Minding Your Business

FedEx Kinkos is a big company, and has long been a presence on TV, either in the form of paid advertisements or as an occasional featured business on news programs and other formats. But then the firm heard about a CNN small-business improvement show called *The Turnaround* (no longer on the air), which traveled across America, introducing troubled small-business owners to high-profile mentors and then helped them develop a plan for success. "When we learned the premise of the show we thought it was a great opportunity to mentor someone using our actual services, and showcase what FedEx Kinkos can do for *all* small businesses at the same time," says Jenny Robertson, manager of marketplace communications for the company.

Ironically, although FedEx Kinkos is a big brand, the show's small-business focus fit perfectly with its strategy to position itself as a small-town, personal, service-oriented solution for entrepreneurs. "We want to be like the Starbucks for small businesses—where owners meet each other while getting their mailings, printings, and packaging done," she says. And being able to convey that feeling in a one-hour show devoted to your brand and dedicated to your message, well, that was an extraordinary opportunity. "One that doesn't come around very often, so when they do you have to be ready to move," according to Jenny.

The company had been looking for ways to showcase everything FedEx Kinkos can provide a small operation without space for operations—from the freelance writer toiling away in their dining room to an Internet start-up bursting out of their garage to a newly minted storeowner. "We really become a small business's 'back office' because we can help them with so many day-to-day tasks like printing anything and everything from banners to business cards, and mailing packages of all shapes and sizes."

On FedEx Kinkos' episode of *The Turnaround*, they worked with a dry cleaning business that was having some trouble. They sent some senior managers out to the store in Dallas, Texas, and worked with the owner on such issues as scheduling, quality control, customer service, marketing advice, and general sales tips. "Actually, there are a lot of similarities between a dry cleaner and what we do, so it was a really great fit," says Jenny. It turned out to be a great experience, as well as a big commitment of time in terms of the managers who traveled to Dallas to work with the dry cleaner and complete the filming. Time well spent, according to the company. "It helped us tell a true story about what the company actually does, through the eyes of CNN and the dry cleaner, and that is so much better than anything the company could say about itself," says the firm's spokesperson. The hour-long show also demonstrated what the firm does on a broad strategic level, and it positioined it as having savvy executive mangement.

Jenny says it was a good decision to put in the time to make the show happen. "It definitely was very successful at generating buzz. We got many calls for our CEO to speak in front of business groups, and it raised his level of visibility in a very positive way." So happy was FedEx Kinkos with the results that they have continued to pursue other television appearances that can boost their positioning as the small-town business and start-up businessperson's best friend. For example, FedEx Kinkos recently taped a fun segment in one of the midtown Manhattan locations with the hosts of *The Morning Show with Mike and Juliet*. The segment was called "Meet Our Neighbors," which introduced the viewing audience to the area where Mike Jerrick and Juliet Huddy film their live daytime talk show. "That was perfect too—we want to be your neighbor, your hometown back office," says Jenny.

Star Power

Weight management service firm Jenny Craig has long used celebrities as spokespeople. Case in point, the recent campaign with actress Kirstie Alley. "Kirstie appeals to so many people, because a lot of us grew up with her on *Cheers, Star Trek, Look Who's Talking,* or *Veronica's Closet*," says Cozette Phifer, spokesperson for Jenny Craig. "Our target audience is thirty-five to forty-two, but she has helped expand our reach. She actually skews younger to the twenty-five-year-old group, but the forty-five to fifty group also responds to her."

One of the advantages of working with a celebrity spokesperson is that it is a news story in and of itself (this can backfire, of course, but more on that later). Jenny Craig created a bold campaign that required Kirstie to lose weight. The business and advertising press covered that story, as did entertainment news programs. Many celebrity and women's magazines covered the fact that Kirstie actually did lose a lot of weight, and these stories in turn were picked up by television programs. When Kirstie appears on shows to talk about her film and television projects, she always talks about her amazing transformation—and mentions Jenny Craig when possible. Even if she doesn't, people are very aware of the connection.

Cozette explains that both Kirstie and Jenny Craig were willing to do something a weight management company had never done before: "After *Veronica's Closet* ended Kirstie was at home with her children and had ended a relationship so she took solace with cooking and baking. I have to applaud her and her team because traditionally you keep a celebrity or any weight loss success story under wraps until they lose the weight. She came out in January saying, 'I'm fat and I need help.' Very daring. No one in weight loss says the F word."

Jenny Craig works closely with the entertainment press, part of the benefit of having a celebrity spokesperson. "Celebrity magazines and shows would not have covered us before," observes Cozette. "Kirstie has had three *People* magazine covers in one year and she was in the hundred most beautiful issue. We did not make that happen. But we do try to place stories whenever she hits a landmark, because for every ten pounds you lose there are such positive health implications you can talk about." If there is a new paparazzi shot of Kirstie, or she has a new exercise, the company lets producers know there are images available.

Jenny Craig gave *Entertainment Tonigh*t an early look of the famous "Pool Boy" commercial to help create a buzz about it. "They run a commercial in its entirety as a new story," says Cozette, who is always working on new angles the press can cover, such as features from noncelebrity Jenny Craig clients. "For example, *ET* interviewed nonprofessionals on what it was like to work with Kirstie—and it turned out to be a really fun and humorous segment."

Jenny Craig creates celebrity connections to their products in other ways. "We work with craft services (the companies that provide food for TV and movie sets), and some of our food is backstage at a lot of shows, including *American Idol* and award programs. We also give celebrities a complimentary in exchange for a mention when the press asks them how they lost their weight. This is a very effective strategy." For example, *The Insider*'s Lara Spencer and *The King of Queens*'s Leah Remini lost their baby weight with Jenny Craig—and they say so when asked.

The Kirstie Alley campaign and other celebrity strategies have paid off for Jenny Craig. But you don't pick winners like them out of a hat. Like many companies, Jenny Craig does surveys asking consumers who they would most like to see in their program. Cozette says, "We narrow it down to about five people and we study their reliability, likability, believability, and trustworthiness." Cozette also believes in intercepts, which is actually stopping someone on the street or in the mall and asking what they think. "They are very instructive, and the person feels flattered and helpful."

There are also dangers involved in having a celebrity spokesperson. Anything can happen because celebrities are real people with flaws and emotions. Anything illegal, immoral, or "wrong place, wrong time" can be detrimental to your company. Sometimes you have to pull a celebrity, like Jenny Craig did with Monica Lewinsky, because people did not respond to her, and cut your losses. Kobe Bryant was scheduled to promote "Kobe's Favorite Spread" when allegations (now dropped) of sexual misconduct surfaced. Whoopi Goldberg was very outspoken about President Bush, and Slim-Fast pulled her, but she now pitches for L.A. Weight Loss.

Cozette recommends disassociating your company from the parts of a person that could be a liability and focus on the good. If you do pick the wrong person you have to react quickly and be ready to go to plan B. Always have another celebrity in the wings who is ready to step in. "At any given time we have fifty to one hundred celebrities on the program and they could become spokespeople if necessary," says Cozette.

Repeat Recognition

"In a mass-market world, oversaturation is a great thing," says Lauren Snyder of Kerzner International. Companies and brands need frequently recurring exposure to make a lasting impression in consumers' minds. There is just too much out there distracting people to get them to focus on something they have seen, read, or heard about only a couple of times. How do you do it? Product placement in "roundup" gift or seasonal segments and giveaways, which we have discussed, are great ways to create brand recognition.

Getting mentions in newspapers and magazines helps build consumer awareness. A Web presence is essential, too. Yet it's hard to drive thousands of people to your site without telling them about it; secure multiple TV segments, place numerous well-timed mentions in magazines and newspapers, and be part of abundant product placements in giveaways and gift-giving segments entirely on your own. There are three resources that help you score multiple impressions, a satellite media tour (SMT), a public relations company, and branding specialists.

Smart Tour

A satellite media tour, or SMT, is a series of prebooked one-on-one interviews with local and national TV stations and electronic outlets across the country and sometimes the world that allows you or your spokesperson to stay in one location. It enables broad television exposure without travel expense for trips that city-to-city media tours require. Basically, you sit in a TV studio with a small camera crew (supplied by the tour company) and do interview after interview. It is cost-effective for companies, but it does come at a price, so it is something an individual would most likely not do unless he or she is flush with cash: about $8,000 to $10,000 per SMT. A satellite radio tour is much more affordable (but works essentially the same way); at about $3,500 it might be something worth investing in, especially if you are an author with a book to sell.

Linda Oken, from Satellite Media Group, one of the premier SMTs, says a company like hers knows what local stations are interested in and they develop story lines for their clients that producers and syndicated and national news feeds are interested in. "One interview sometimes leads to multiple airings if you are doing the interview with a major network such as ABC News 1, which can be picked up by numerous regional ABC stations—via satellite," she explains.

Linda says the most successful SMTs are those that localize and tailor pitches appropriately. "A lot of local stations only air material that is of interest to their region, so an energy conservation expert may be better positioned to do an SMT in cold weather markets. An expert or brand that targets older people does better in Florida, Arizona, Palm Springs, and similar retirement markets," she says.

"Of course, national morning shows or afternoon talk programs are major outlets, and appearances on those shows can have immediate impact on sales," says Linda, "but it could be hit or miss, too. Going local with news you can use helps build wide recognition with a very specific, sympathetic, and motivated audience." That's because local shows are often considered "destination TV," while national TV shows are sometimes background noise to other activities.

Like any other appearance, an SMT can't be too commercial. Television news shows are very concerned that SMTs not appear to be selling something outright. Some will do 'sponsored stories,' with a clear statement that the segment has been paid for by the company featured in the segment, but that's the exception. So, for example, it might be difficult for a pharmaceutical company to book an SMT to talk about health issues. An independent health expert or physician-author may have an easier time. "Books and authors inherently are not commercial, so they make ideal candidates for the SMT," says Linda. Plus, local bookers love authors and books, especially if the topic or author offers a regional connection.

The other exciting aspect of an SMT is that you can time it to run in conjunction with certain events or times of year. "A time hook is useful because if the book or idea or product can be tied into Father's Day or National Humor Month, it compels stations to use the interview in a timely fashion. Sometimes stations sit on an interview for months waiting for an opening—so timely hooks are something that helps get it out there fast," she advises.

Linda wants clients she can trust, who are articulate, good on air, and have something more to offer than just a talking head. "It goes without saying that television is a visual medium, and stations hesitate to book something that offers no visual excitement. We always try to shoot B-roll or in-the-field material to make segments more dynamic."

When selecting an SMT firm, Linda advises hiring someone with a demonstrable track record of television bookings and good relationships with stations and producers (including testimonials). Check references and make sure their client list matches your areas of expertise. Some companies specialize in certain topics or products (Linda is particularly experienced with books and authors).

If you cannot afford an SMT, Linda says the new media landscape has opened up new horizons. "Recently, publishing companies have started to do streaming videos that are shown over the Web, and relating to that they are specifically developing electronic press kits that can be played online or downloaded onto a computer," she says. The audience is not as big as for TV, but developments on the Internet are growing, as are the number of sites that use streaming video.

"CBS news.com is very interested in a range of stories, and ABC does live Internet that you can download to your iPod," says Linda. That represents a whole new world of distribution outlets, and since streaming videos are available for a longer time, yours has a very long shelf life—almost indefinite. "It's really new and who knows where it might go." Plus, Linda says, you can pitch streaming videos yourself, directly to the online news outlets.

The PR Machine

Public relations provide credibility that you do not get from advertising. Years ago PR was about sending out press releases, but the practice is so far advanced from that now. If you have not figured it out by now, this book is really about how to be your own publicity agent. But you can do only so much. You may reach a point where someone dedicated to the profession comes in handy or may be necessary to keep up with demand or increase your exposure. The PR field is vast and varied. Publicists specialize in everything from books to fashion and beauty to politics to celebrity and entertainment. When considering hiring a PR person, make sure he or she understands your business and brand.

You may be fabulous, but your PR person might suck. Make it your business to know what your PR person is saying about your brand, and how they are pitching it. We have been pitched segments where we thought, Hmm, that could have been a good idea, but the PR person doesn't know what they are talking about, so forget it. Get to know the PR person's reputation and style before you sign him or her on.

PR pros can be hired on a project basis or on retainer (generally a set fee paid monthly). Bigger agencies can charge from $10,000 to $20,000 a month; smaller firms may charge $2,000 to $5,000 a month. Either way, it is an investment, so make sure yours is working hard for you. Ask for monthly reports, and if you are not getting media placements after six or eight weeks, reevaluate your relationship. Terence once received a book "pitch" from an expensive PR agent consisting of a Xeroxed press release written by the publisher. That is *not* the kind of PR you want to pay for—you can do better yourself.

Recently he called a PR person at a spa resort—no call back. How would you feel if you were paying a PR person and they didn't return phone calls from television producers, or anyone, for that matter?

You could be the easiest person to work with but your PR person could be difficult and that makes you difficult in the minds of producers. Check in regularly and find out who they called or talked to each week and what their pitches looked like. It is so important. It never ceases to amaze us when a PR person says no to a request that their client be part of a segment, that they will do it only if the segment is all about them. We almost laugh when we hear that—that doesn't happen unless it is a paid segment. We feel sorry for companies and experts that use bad PR people. You have to be in charge of your own destiny.

Lippe Taylor's Charly Rok further advises that you hire someone who uses your brand or "lives and breathes it." If they are not enthusiastic on a personal level their pitches just won't be as compelling. Another advantage is an agency with a diverse client base, even if they specialize in a certain area, such as lifestyle or fashion. "How many times can you pitch the same story to the same producers? If I have a plethora of accounts there is always something enticing for a producer, and I can find a way to work more than one client into a pitch," she says.

"When I worked with Jenny Craig I learned that many of their clients who lost weight became employees; when I worked with David's Bridal I saw that many customers also became employees, so I pitched a story about loyal customers becoming employees and it was picked up," she says. That's why you pay a PR agent: to think beyond the boundaries of your brand

and get you worked in to a variety of stories in new and interesting ways. "Sometimes it's not a big mention, or a piece gets bumped or cut, but in volume it does make an impression on viewers or editors and producers, so it is a matter of educating the client as to the importance of being included in a variety of media."

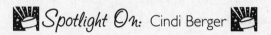

Spotlight On: Cindi Berger

If anyone deserves the prefix "über" before their job title, it's public relations pro Cindi Berger, a partner with PMK/HBH Public Relations in New York. Cindi represents such celebrities as Sharon Stone, Rosie O'Donnell, the Dixie Chicks, and many others. Rarely interviewed, she sat down with us to share her perspective on what a great PR firm can do for your brand or message.

Starring You!: What's your PR philosophy?
Cindi Berger: Our philosophy is that publicity is done for a reason; it's not just to see your name or face on TV. Each campaign must be tailored for the specific target audience. We use television for publicity when there is a specific reason to do it, whether it is a film or TV project an actor has, or a book or a play. PR campaigns are always geared and tailored to a specific project.

SY: Any specific success stories from past corporate (brand) clients?
CB: We handled John Travolta's surprise birthday party at Palmilla Resort to coincide with their opening. A multipart deal was orchestrated, which involved vari-

ous *GMA* crews covering it in a controlled way. It was a private party with many celebrities in attendance, such as Oprah, Barbra Streisand, and Tom Cruise. It is still a private birthday party at what is now considered to be one of the top resorts in the world, we can offer the excitement of the resort and the party through a controlled PR campaign that included a spread in *In Style* magazine and a multipart story on *GMA,* so it was huge and the word spread, and it is still sold out so the demand really arose out of the unbelievable launch for the resort. The way various media platforms worked together made it an exciting celebrity-oriented editorial story for the print and TV press.

SY: *You get a huge bang for your buck from TV, though, because of its reach.*
CB: Certainly. You access the masses and there are few other ways to do that. We did a Verizon announcement on the *Today* show. It was a news story, the launch of V Cast music. No other phone carrier had done it and the announcement on the *Today* show was done simultaneously with the consumer products show in Las Vegas. That was the start of a huge campaign.

SY: *What's your advice in terms of talking to a producer?*
CB: It's all about having a relationship with the producer. They are more apt to listen to your pitch because the relationship is everything. It is also about who you are able to get on the phone. If the problem is not solved I will call Matt Lauer directly—the best PR people have the ability to get the top people on the phone.

SY: *Dealing with clients?*

CB: You have to manage expectations with your client; you have to educate them and set realistic goals. You want to pitch a story that you believe, in your heart of hearts, that the producer or writer will find interesting. Don't pitch it if it is not realistic. The newest craze is underwater basket weaving, or waterproof lace making will be the next craze—come on! It's an education process. Make them understand that nothing is carved in stone, "no" is never forever. It might be no now but you have to teach clients that rejection today is also part of building a strong relationship with the media. You can call in favors but do it in an elegant way. I do not do that often.

SY: *What advice do you have for people/brands who might be hiring PR? What should a public relations firm look for?*

CB: The most important ingredient is having the gravitas to do the job that the client is asking—it is a collaborative process. I have never been a yes person and I have always told clients what I think. They also have to remember that it takes a long time to build a brand. Even with someone like Sharon Stone. She is the new face for Christian Dior skin care for mature women. She was always proud of the fact that she is honest about her age. It is a building process. *Total Recall* put her on the map. But before *Basic Instinct* opened I told her, 'Your life will never be the same.' That was a big movie that put her at a whole new level in her career. When the movie went to Cannes, she started down the red carpet as an actress and by the time she reached the top of the stairs, she was a movie star. That is to say the media is very powerful. You have to control it as much as you can.

Brand You

Branding is one way to cope with the cost of advertising and still build consumer recognition, whether you have a product or are creating a personality. "When you are at a cocktail party and advertising comes up, the layman thinks of a page in a magazine and a commercial on TV but it is so much more than that now," says Scott Woodward, long-time branding expert and CEO of Sew Branded. (He was the force behind shaping and revitalizing the global image for Ray-Ban sunglasses and branding Calvin Klein around the world, among other brands.)

If you are trying to promote a product, one of the best ways to get a message out to the public is through product or personality placement, says Scott. "Clients who come to us with small budgets have to build their brand in nontraditional ways. If you aren't a nationally known brand or expert, you do not have the luxury of getting a regular gig on a weekly or daily show. So you have to use appearances to build the brand and augment it with product placement. It's critical mass," he advises. So, for example, someone like Scott can help you place your sunglasses on Will Smith's face at a movie premiere. He'll create a story that style editors can write about. Then he will help develop a company spokesperson (or do it himself) to talk about style—when they appear the brand is always mentioned.

Scott points to interior designer Nate Berkus as a person who has built a recognizable brand from his expertise. "Nate is buddies with a producer at *Oprah,* and he is also gorgeous and everyone likes him. He is on *Oprah* twice a month and it's always her number-one rated show," he says. In effect, Nate has taken his small interior design business in Chicago and propelled it into a national business. He has a monthly column on interiors in *Elle*. From there he has built a brand that now includes licensing his name to home accessories. Another textbook example in the same area is Ty Pennington. "He was a model who was not getting gigs," says Scott. So he took his handyman know-how and propelled that into a gig on *Trading Spaces*. (Who would have thought that it would be the carpenter on the show who would become its biggest success story?) Now he has a hit network show and a deal with Sears. "Ty is branded, there is no question about it," says Scott.

The best way to control the media is by becoming part of it—as a paid consultant or expert or even as a host or creator of your own show. It's not for everyone, but why not dream big? The next big hit could be "starring you"!

 ## It's a Wrap

- Treat producers like confidants: give them scoops and access to the latest news and info from your area of expertise.
- Make yourself available and dependable—that way producers will think of you first when they need to book a segment.
- Start thinking of yourself or your business as a brand.
- Be honest with yourself. If you are not the best spokesperson for your brand, find someone who is.

Chapter 7

Show You the Money

Sometimes a guest is so compelling and appealing to the audience that he or she starts appearing regularly on shows, turning up everywhere from morning networks to cable news to daytime talk. Producers and show runners realize, Hey, this person is a believable expert whom viewers respond to and we want them all to ourselves. The only way they can do that is to hire the guest as a paid on-air consultant or contributor (it is unlikely you will appear on competing shows during your term of contract). Short of having your own show (see chapter eight), being paid for your expertise or commentary is the holy grail most TV experts want to reach.

Don't make the mistake of thinking you will get rich by becoming a paid expert; but you may become rich from the after-affects of being a professional expert because your business, if you have one, may soar. Most paid experts earn standard rates, based on the American Federation of Television & Radio Artists (AFTRA, www.aftra.org) scale. Rates change slightly every year or so, but per appearance rates range from the low to mid hundreds of dollars per episode. Sometimes you can negotiate more, depending on your experience and popularity. Hot commodities always have greater earning and bargaining potential. As your name becomes more established, with an agent/manager behind you, you can negotiate a greater fee.

We want to make a distinction between the paid expert and a host of a show. Paid experts still focus on their expertise and business; TV is a vehicle to promote or expand that business or brand. A paid on-air expert often has a career in a particular field (which is what makes him or her an expert) and contributes to a network or a specific show on a regular but not full-time basis. Behind-the-scenes experts generally come from a professional background and make a transition to television and bring their knowledge with them, as in the case of a food stylist, a makeup person, or a medical person who consults, writes for, or advises shows that need medical expertise. Police officers and lawyers also serve in a similar capacity. A host is someone who makes a career of being on television as the lead personality on a show, or a show is specifically created around his or her personality and expertise. We talk about these people in the next chapter.

Is there a secret formula for making the leap? Well, yes. It's the same one we have shared with you in the previous six chapters. All the reasons that a producer would want to book you as a guest are the same reasons a show or network would want to hire you as an expert:

1. A well-defined message or brand
2. An appealing "look"
3. The ability to express credible, reliable information crisply and articulately

4. Energy (see chapter five), but with the volume turned up

5. Information you have that no one else has or no one can express as well as you can

6. **Being good at what you do.** This is important, and sounds obvious, but once you forget your expertise and start focusing on being on TV is when you start to lose your appeal. Believe us when we tell you that we have seen people crash and burn for this reason time and time again. Plus, being prominent in your field gives you a dramatic edge—your access to inside information in your area is a huge selling point.

Getting noticed by talent execs, producers, and talent agents who have the power to put you on-air or get you a contract is the number-one way to make the transition from TV volunteer (guest) to wage earner. **That is exactly why you have to make every appearance count—everyone in the industry watches television specifically looking for people who could be their next paid consultant, contributor, or host.** We are always watching the shows to see if there is anyone we should meet or who has the potential to go to the next level as a professional or who has a brand that can be developed. Mark Turner, an agent with more than twelve years of experience in the host/ broadcast division of the Abrams Artists Agency in New York City (you'll hear more from him in chapter eight), specializes in experts and hosts in the areas of therapy, self-help, relationships, lifestyle, and interior design. He says that like all TV agents and development people, he always has his eye on the screen. "If I see a psychologist on *Good Morning America*, and they're really good, I try to meet them," he says.

You don't have to have a particular kind of expertise to get paid for sharing it. There are all sorts of specialist contributors on television—from ex–military personnel who comment on war to former presidential candidates who give the insiders' perspective on Washington to stylists who discuss the latest fashion and design trends. There are even craft and food science experts who, yes, get paid to consult on craft and cooking shows, and who even appear on air. You can have an amazing television career—and you don't necessarily have to quit your "day job" (although some do, especially those who end up working behind the scenes).

Here's an assignment: Create a professional expert package. Create a reel or disk with your best (and most recent) TV appearances. If you do not have many appearances, create a mock interview with a video camera to supplement the reel. Next, create a one-page résumé that explains who you are and what topics you have talked about with authority. Make a bulleted list of other topics you feel confident you can talk about. Wrap it up with any sample work (including any published articles or books). Keep it snappy and short. Make several copies so it's ready to go when a producer shows interest in your skills or knowledge.

There are all kinds of expert consulting deals that can be made—there really is no standard fee or financial arrangement. What you get paid and for how long have to do with what kind of show you are on and what kind of budget the show has. A network news show pays a military or political consultant more than a lifestyle network pays a knitting expert. We cannot help you negotiate a deal—if someone offers you a job as a paid consultant you need an entertainment lawyer to help you negotiate a fair contract. You may not need an agent or a manager at this stage, but most paid consultants seek the help of an attorney in coming to terms with a fair deal for everyone.

The best way for you to learn about becoming a TV expert is to listen to the stories of people who have done it—on both sides of the camera. Many of them continue working in the career that brought them to television in the first place. We also talk to pros who have brought their knowledge behind the camera. As far as we are concerned, they qualify as paid experts, too. No matter what your specialty, the advice and stories of these people have universal application. All of the on-air experts started first as unpaid guests, and many used *local* TV to get their start.

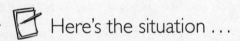 Here's the situation . . .

Experts are paid to be experts, not to produce

If you become a paid expert, please keep in mind that this does not mean you know better or more about the show than the producer or director. You don't. When a host or expert starts telling a producer how to do his job it's the kiss of death—for the expert. It's very annoying and it does not make us predisposed to renew your contract.

Terence

Political Party! Fred Barnes and Tucker Carlson

Turn on any cable news show at almost any hour and you will see what, in the business, we call talking heads (THs) debating everything from the war in Iraq to the First Amendment (our favorite one) to Washington scandals (always plenty of these to go around). When the host of these shows identifies THs as "contributors" that means they are being paid for sharing their views on air. Political consultants or experts come from an assortment of backgrounds, the most common being former politicians, former political speechwriters, communications professionals, and print journalists and op-ed writers.

Tucker Carlson and Fred Barnes are two journalists who have made the leap from scribe to consultant to host. Like many experts who have brought their knowledge to the small screen, they did so primarily by "sticking to their knitting" and as a result, got noticed by TV. No matter what side of the political spectrum you fall on, there is no denying that these guys are skilled debaters and can present their side in an articulate, energetic way. That's why TV likes them.

Fred Barnes cohosts *The Beltway Boys* and is a regular contributor to *Special Report with Brit Hume* on Fox Cable News Network. He also appears as chief correspondent on the PBS series *National Desk*. Fred was also the senior editor and White House correspondent for *The New Republic*, and a founder and executive editor of *The Weekly Standard*. Plus, he hosts two weekly radio shows, *Issues in the News* on Voice of America and *What's the Story*.

Fred's TV career started in 1984, when he was "an obscure reporter in Baltimore writing about politics." He would occasionally be asked to appear on *The McLaughlin Group*, a public affairs show. "I had never seen the show, but some of my friends were on it, so I knew it would be a relatively big step for me. I was flattered and seized the opportunity," he says.

In 1988 one of the regular panelists, Robert Novak, left

for CNN and Fred took his place for ten years. "I got along with McLaughlin, which was no small feat, and once again I accepted instantly. I tell young people to accept all invitations even if it is an obscure program. Then when you are being questioned by Tim Russert on *Meet the Press* you will be used to the camera, and you'll be grooving," he counsels. "The first thing the bookers at Fox ask me when I recommend a guest is, What has he or she been on? They do not want someone who freezes when the red light goes on."

Fred can get his message out to a greater number of people via TV, but he says as a political writer, being on TV gives him greater access to key people and invitations to background briefings. Those interested in being political experts or panelists on TV would be well advised to get their commentary published in the right places. "There's a good chance you will get on a show if you write for any national publication, or if you write in Washington," he says. If you write for papers that are not circulated in Washington, you can e-mail articles that have a national angle to the bookers at Fox or TV producers at other news programs. "The bookers at Fox don't have time to read the *Chicago Tribune*. But if you get picked up in a Web digest like www.realclearpolitics.com, which they do read, you will be on their radar," advises Fred.

In terms of handling the sometimes vitriolic, fast-paced patter that takes place on political or issue-oriented shows, Fred urges: make yourself known. "You cannot wait to be called on and one way to make sure is to slide to the end of your seat [inserting yourself physically into the group]. It's easier to have your say." If you are seated at a panel where you are seen from the waist up, leaning forward with your hands and forearms on the table has the same effect.

The other advice Fred offers is one we've been drumming into you and is *so* important when you are talking about political opinions, which can easily become muddled and confused if you aren't focused. Preparation. **"You want to be in control of what you are saying. Know the subject matter and organize specific thoughts beforehand. Stick to one idea.** If you try to get more than one idea into the conversation you will get the producer's signal to cut it off. And you'll confuse people. The one way to get in more than one idea is to set it up: 'There are three reasons to stay in Lebanon and they are . . .'" he says. To get away with that technique, you have to be very practiced.

Fred says once you're on TV, smile a lot and keep *yourself* in perspective. People will think you are a nice person even if you aren't. "People don't like grumpy, sour reporters who tend to take themselves way too seriously. Realize you do not know everything. Politics is art and not science. Journalists who think they are smarter than the people they cover make a mistake because they're not. You don't know more than they do, and it's not good to exude that idea on TV," he counsels.

Tucker is the host of *Tucker* on MSNBC. Previously, he was the host and managing editor of PBS's *Tucker Carlson: Unfiltered* and before that he was the youngest host in CNN history, first on *The Spin Room*, and then on *Crossfire*. Before becoming a TV personality, he wrote about national affairs and politics for newspapers and magazines. He continues to writer regularly for *Esquire*—and he's even been a contestant on *Dancing with the Stars*.

Before CNN signed him, however, he would appear on a TV show called *Inside Politics* to talk about current political issues because of his provocative essays in national magazines and newspapers. Then one day everything changed (as often happens in the world of TV). "It was 2000 and I was working for Tina Brown's *Talk* magazine, covering the election. I got a call from CNN asking me if I wanted to host a special on the Lieberman-Cheney debate with Bill Press and I said, Yes, why not?" recalls Tucker. It was a pretty slapdash production, which turned out to be a good test of the host's skills. "It was so unplanned the teleprompter said 'ad lib here' at certain points," says Tucker. Despite that fact, the show got huge numbers and CNN called Tucker the next day to offer him a job. He's been on TV ever since, for six years.

Now that he has made the shift from pundit to host he has some great suggestions for would-be TV political experts—or any expert, for that matter. "If you are self-conscious or are overly impressed with TV, you won't do well. Larry King gave me the best piece of advice—he said you should care, but not too much," Tucker advises. Translated, that means having no fear—it kills you on TV.

In terms of what he looks for in a political expert today, it's someone who can speak and explain things in a way that viewers can understand. "Energetic, picturesque language that is evocative and compelling," he says. Knowing what the issues are is a given, and that means keeping up with newspapers, magazines, and political blogs, since producers get a lot of their ideas from print sources. "The Drudge Report is the assignment editor for a lot of these shows," says Tucker.

One of the "signatures" of a lot of political shows is the screaming match. Producers purposely schedule two people who represent opposing sides hoping a fight will result—and it often does. What should you do if you are going on air to face off with a political opponent? Like Fred, he says, "Always remain calm—getting mad never works on TV, ever," says

Tucker. If the other person is talking over you and the host is not intervening (as he should), he recommends saying, "I let you speak, now allow me to speak," and then do not give up. "After three times of asking, if they are still talking just keep on making your point even if you are talking at the same time," he says. Finally, he says humor always wins political arguments. "Fifteen seconds of wit are worth more than fifteen minutes of bile and rhetoric. If you can say something funny and make your point you win, it's over, no one can beat you."

Fred and Tucker are perfect examples of our theory, say yes and figure it out later. We love that they never gave an invitation to be on TV a second thought, and the audience for their written work has become much more substantial because of it.

Legal Eagle: Joe Tacopina

There are numerous crime and legal shows on television; in fact, there is an entire network devoted to criminal cases: Court TV. Every one of them needs lawyers, detectives, and former judges to act as consultants and on-air commentators. But not just anyone makes the grade. Joe Tacopina is one of the most sought-after experts in the business, and until recently he was a legal correspondent for ABC (he had to resign because many of the high-profile cases he would have commented on he was actually involved in as a lawyer). Putting in about ten hours a year, he says he gets paid three times as much as he did when he started out in the Brooklyn district attorney's office working eighty hours a week for $35,000 a year.

Being a legal consultant on TV also helps his practice as one of the country's foremost defense attorneys. For instance, Maureen St. Guillen, the mother of Imette, a young woman in New York who was abducted and murdered, allegedly by a bouncer at a New York City bar, hired Joe to represent the young woman's family in a civil lawsuit against the bouncer and his employer after seeing him passionately argue on behalf of his client Juran van der Sloot and his father. "I am not known for plaintiff cases but Maureen saw me on TV arguing on my client's behalf and she wanted someone to passionately advance her agenda and defend her daughter Imette," he explains.

His path to TV expert started in the Brooklyn prosecutor's office. "I left because I started having children [he has five] and I could not afford to work there," he says. Joe literally hung out a shingle in 1994. "I rented one of those office packages where you get a mailbox and a conference room and they answer the phones for you. I would make calls at a diner for two hours every day." He made his first career mark when he won an acquittal for police officer Thomas Weise, one of four officers charged in Brooklyn Federal Court with the infamous precinct house torture of Haitian immigrant Abner Louima, in 1997. "I said a few words outside of court and I was on page one of the [New York] *Times*. Then I got a call from NY1, Court TV, and then Fox News so that's how my relationship with TV started. I got on the Geraldo circuit—he was a pioneer of the legal talk show," he says.

TV appearances were not all seamless for Joe. The first time he was on Court TV was legal pro Dan Abrams's first hosting gig. "It was probably the worst hour of TV ever. I refused to look up and I had written all these notes and I was afraid to move off my notes and Abrams was reading the teleprompter. The producers said it was fine but it wasn't," he recalls. Practice makes perfect, however.

"**The more you go on the more you become a regular.** Old school lawyers told me I was making a huge mistake going on TV but I did not agree," he says. "It is a different era now. TV in conjunction with a real practice is for a lawyer a great way to get your expertise and point of view out to people." Joe cautions would-be TV lawyers to focus on their practices and to strike a balance in terms of being on TV all the time. "It looks like you have nothing to do. For me, TV is a hobby. I have filled in for Dan Abrams and had fun with it and I have been offered my own show and that's exciting. Maybe someday but not right now; I like being a lawyer for cases I believe in."

For lawyers out there who do want to make the leap, Joe says you need to establish your identity first (see chapter two) and then get known for a case so you have credibility. "I have seen lawyers try for years to get on TV; they hire people to help them, but the point is, it takes a lot of luck to catch some breaks and you have to be good at your job."

Joe's experience makes a perfect "case" for how TV can improve your business. Word of mouth from happy clients is one thing, but the credibility that being a TV expert gives you clients and business from all over the world, from people who would have limited access to you otherwise.

 Here's the situation …

Don't take TV jobs and relationships casually

We recently worked with a stylist to whom we had given a lot of television opportunities. She was scheduled to work as the host of a new show and then backed out of it at the last minute when she got a contributor job on another new show. We found out later that she now thought she was a star and had become very demanding. Contributors and paid experts aren't stars until they are hosts of their own shows. There are three lessons here. First, you can't go from 0 to 120 overnight, and it's a recipe for disaster to think and act like you can. Second, you have to remember who you are. Experts are easily replaced and a bad attitude will not help you. There are many people who do the same thing who can take your place in an instant. Finally, who is to say that one of us won't be working on her show a year from now—or on the next show she wants to work on. Because TV is such a small world we would not be surprised if that were the case.

Terence

Money Talks: Terry Savage

Every network and news show also has at least one finance and money expert. Most of these people are actually in the business, and work as money managers, financial consultants, or heads of brokerage houses. Sometimes they are financial reporters who have made the transition to TV. Terry Savage, for example, is a nationally known expert on personal finance and a regular television commentator on CNN, CNBC, PBS, and NBC. She is also a nationally syndicated personal finance columnist and an author. In fact, one of her best sellers, *The Savage Truth on Money*, was made into an hour-long PBS special.

Terry started her career as a stockbroker, and was a founding member and the first woman trader on the Chicago Board Options Exchange. Her first TV experience came in the 1970s, on a *local* stock market station in Chicago. "I was unique as a woman on the floor and I was doing well. Local channel 26 asked me if I would do a show for an hour a day. We called it *Terry's Time*. I sent a tape from that show to NBC in Chicago. It was just a long shot, but at the time interest rates were moving up and down and the markets were crazy and it was not just rich people who were interested in investing. NBC hired me based on that crazy little tape!" she says. Yet more proof that it pays to do local TV, dear readers.

Every afternoon Terry would go to the station and talk about the market and what it meant to regular people. Since she worked on the floor of the market, she had her ear to the ground of what was happening. That inside information made her a valuable commentator. "I was trading interest rate futures at the Mercantile and the interest rates on certificates of deposit [CDs] changed every Tuesday morning. The new rate was based on the treasury bill auction that took place Monday at twelve thirty, but the results were never announced until 7 P.M. Monday, after the banks closed.

"Because of my job I knew at twelve thirty within a couple of percentages of a point what the rate would be the next day so I would come to NBC Chicago at noon on Monday and call my friends on the trading floor at twelve twenty, so that right after the sports report and before the cute closing story I could tell viewers what the interest rates would probably be the next day so they would know whether to renew their CD or withdraw it." Today, of course, such information is recorded instantly and everyone knows about it, but then Terry had significant information that regular people would not have had easy access to without her.

That was just the beginning for Terry. Eventually she had

her own local (there's that word again) morning talk show and later she moved to doing evening news segments. She got the attention of the editor of the *Chicago Sun-Times* and got a column in 1987, which was eventually syndicated all over the country, bringing her greater recognition. "After the column had been in the papers for a number of years I was approached by a publisher to turn them into a book, which I did with *Terry Savage Talks Money.*"

TV seems to come naturally to Terry (admittedly this is not the case with everyone) but despite that fact, she does not see it as an end in itself. "It's a medium through which I touch people. I assume you can learn how to be good, and people take courses in it, but for me it was a natural thing. The lens of the camera disappears and I am not focused on it," she says, echoing Tucker Carlson's advice about not being overly impressed with the camera or being fearful of it. "I think there is a woman peeling potatoes at the kitchen counter and I want to get her attention. I am talking to her as an individual and that helps me forget about the camera once I start talking," says Terry.

Being an "insider" like Terry and Joe, no matter what your field, is what makes you an appealing paid expert candidate.

Here's an assignment: make a list of information you can or have access to (legally, of course) that would make you a valuable contributor to a show. This is different from the list you made earlier of topics you are conversant in. This is information that can make a difference in viewers' lives and can earn you a paying gig.

The lesson we hope you learn from Terry's story is: *go local.* Those short appearances on small stations gave her enviable TV, publishing, and public-speaking career its start. After reading this story we don't know how anyone could possibly turn up his or her nose at local TV again.

 I have to tell you ...

Experts have to know their stuff inside and out, backward and forward

I want to send up a caution: TV exposes fools mercilessly. If you get a chance to appear on TV to talk about an area of expertise, *be prepared*. Never try to fool the producer—we don't like that. If you are asked to talk about something and you don't think you can that's the one time you should seriously consider passing or offer to talk about something else. Otherwise, you have to make sure you do your research and know the topic backward and forward. As Nancy Grace told us, knowing your stuff is the number-one way to eliminate fear and be successful. Not knowing your stuff is the number-one way to eliminate your face from TV. If you claim to have expertise that you do not have you'll be dancing around for answers you do not know—and that's bad TV.

Marta

Grey's Anatomy: Zoanne Clack

Medical experts are in demand, and not just on news shows where they comment on the latest medical research, health information, and drug trials (lawyers comment on drug companies *on* trial). Denise Cramsey, who helped produce *Medical Detectives* in the late 1990s, says that since medical stories are all research based the best medical experts are needed to give them credibility and reliability. "We found the best medical examiners on that show and many of them have gone on to be very well-known television commentators and regular experts," she says, pointing specifically to Drs. Michael Baden and Henry Lee. "Both have large TV personalities even though they are quite different men. Lee is very quiet and reserved and peaceful and Baden is fiery."

Medical experts are also employed as consultants and writers on scripted medical shows, where accuracy is key since a lot of people get medical information from such shows. Terence's friend Nick, a doctor who works with children, tells the story of meeting with the parents of a two-year-old child with a new diagnosis of leukemia. The meeting with his parents was heavy-duty, but after the tears and explanations (people can discuss big news like that for only so long, according to Nick), he switched gears and asked the parents if they understood the hierarchy of the hospital, especially since they would be spending a lot of time there. They said, "Oh yes, we understand it. . . . After all, we watch *Grey's Anatomy* all the time."

Dr. Zoanne Clack is now a writer and coproducer of the ABC megahit *Grey's Anatomy,* but her TV career got started in ER work—a *real* ER. She spent ten years doing medicine before she caught the TV bug. "I was not finding my niche and I was looking for something to keep me in medicine and I was not finding it," she says. As fate would have it, she was living in Atlanta and started dating a man who lived in Los Angeles. "I visited him there, and the energy and creativity in LA clicked in my head. I thought, I can take my ER shift anywhere, so even though we broke up I moved to LA," she says.

Eventually a friend told her about an ad she had seen in

a Hollywood trade paper —the show *ER* was looking for an on-set adviser. Zoanne sent them a letter and they did not respond. However, she learned later that two of her college mentors trained with the man who was doing the hiring. "So of course I shot off another letter mentioning their names and received a reply immediately." She did not get that job, but she made an impression on the producers she met with. We'll get to that in a minute.

Zoanne continued with her hospital shift work and took evening classes in writing and producing in her free time. "It's a good way to get to know people and learn important skills," she says, because the people who teach night or extension classes usually work in the business. A year and a half later one of the producers she met at her *ER* interview was making her own show, which was called *Presidio Med*. "She was not sure she needed a doctor because they had one, so I was a backup. But as it turned out, two or three months later they hired both of us as staff writers," says Zoanne.

The show was canceled after eight months, but it did not matter. Zoanne still had her shift work and she had written spec scripts (sample scripts for existing shows to demonstrate your skills). She had an agent by now, too (it was not difficult to get one once she had her TV show). "I do not know which spec script they sent, but I got offered two jobs that season, *Grey's* and *House*. I chose *Grey's* because they offered me an increase in status. *House* debuted and it was a huge hit and we were nervous, but the rest is history," she says of what in retrospect was a wise decision. "Use what you have and don't try to hide it—that's what makes you unique and stand out," advises Zoanne. "The biggest compliment I get is when someone in TV meets me and I tell him or her I am a doctor, and they say,

'What?'" she laughs. It's very unexpected to meet a TV writer who is also a doctor. And to keep her fresh and up to date on medicine, Zoanne still does shifts at the ER.

Stylishly Yours: David Evangelista

Beauty experts abound—news and talk shows are always looking for people who can comment on the latest trends and dispense advice to style-challenged viewers. You don't have to be a journalist to be a beauty expert, however, as hairdresser David Evangelista has proved.

David came to New York to try to make it as a stylist with $100 in his pocket. He came from a working-class family in New Jersey, went to beauty school in Philadelphia, and really wanted to work at the Frédéric Fekkai salon. He made something out of nothing but talent and hope. Now he has a deal with *The Early Show* on CBS that guarantees him a certain number of paid appearances per year. He is a five-time Emmy Award nominee for his work as television hairstylist for *The Rosie O'Donnell Show.* He has also appeared on the show *Life & Style* and as a judge on the CBS reality show *Wickedly Perfect,* and he cohosts a show on the TV Guide Channel.

David does everything he can to keep himself on air. In addition to all the work he does in the States, he also hosts a show in Canada. Canada can be a good market for lifestyle shows and they are often picked up in the States and developed into American versions for the U.S. market. Yes, he makes money at it, but the consistent exposure he gets is more valuable for his long-term plans. David still does roundup shows on VH1 and E! for free, and he is more than willing to sit for two hours to be on air for thirty seconds.

"I see myself as a brand," says David. "My background is in beauty and fashion. I can style hair, apply makeup, and style clothing. That makes me fluent in the three major areas of the beauty and fashion world, which translates to a bevy of different kinds of TV appearances." It occurred to David to brand himself as a professional expert after producers on TV shows encouraged him to do so. He advises beauty and fashion pros who want to work on TV to develop and focus on a message. "Your message should be what you eat, breathe, sleep, and live by," he says. Resist the temptation to listen to people who tell you what you should be or who you are, particularly people who are not in your business or in the television business. "You know yourself and what you are capable of. Believe in it," he says.

Fashion and beauty experts have to be very conscious of their audience, according to David. They know when you are talking down to them, and for a beauty expert that's a bad thing because it is such a personal, intimate subject that people at home can feel very insecure about. "I never want to or will be disrespectful to my audience. I strive to empower my audience every time I am on television," he says. Those who don't will never make it as a paid expert.

Beauty experts also have a unique opportunity to cross promote themselves. David says his business strategy is to build on opportunities that come his way. "For instance, being on *The Early Show* allows me to promote my hair salon. Being written up in a magazine like *Entertainment Weekly* allows me to promote a TV show I am hosting," he says. "It's all about building my brand."

The Travel Mom: Emily Kaufman

Emily Kaufman has a background in early childhood development and education. She was teaching and wanted to share information with other parents. She branded and pitched herself to local and national TV as "Commando Mom" because she realized that moms want to hear from other moms when it comes to parenting advice. "My pieces were from the perspective of a real mother who was raising a son and daughter but with a professional background. I would do segments on miserable but common problems such as having a civil dinner out with the kids or trying to get them to bed at night," she says.

Everything changed for Emily when a publicist from a Big Bear, California, hotel asked her to do her parenting segments from the kid-friendly resort. "I had information on taking road trips and I pitched a show called *Travel Daily* to the Travel Channel. Then it occurred to me that there must be no one available to talk about kids and travel so I trademarked The Travel Mom, and created a Web site. I wanted to own the niche of talking about traveling with kids," she says.

Emily didn't set out to make a career of The Travel Mom, but it turned out that way. She's now a corporate media spokesperson and author (*The Travel Mom's Ultimate Book of Family Travel*). She started out as a teacher doing segments on local TV. One of her secrets for getting booked was to deliver budget-friendly reports, because she says the average American family does not stay at the Four Seasons—they stay at the Red Roof Inn. "I show people how to make travel accessible, and it was going great, and then 9/11 hit and I thought, That's it, it's over." But the catastrophe actually opened the world of the corporate spokesperson to her. Travel and hospitality companies were worried that no one would want to travel, especially with children, and they had to find ways to reassure people.

"The hospitality industry thought that if they put The Travel Mom in a particular location people would see it was okay to travel," she explains. She works with Hilton Hotels, car rental companies, Coppertone, Orbitz, and Disney as a media expert on family travel. She has appeared on numerous TV shows, including *The View*, *GMA*, Fox News, and many others. She has become the "mother of all travel."

In terms of becoming a professional expert Emily believes, like we do, that the worst thing anyone can say to you is "no." That's not so bad—you just keep trying. "You have to believe in yourself and position yourself as an authority. I say to shows, You need me because no one at your show is a mom; I say to hotel chains and travel companies, I am important because you need to be talking to families and mothers. I tell *Woman's Day* and other magazines, You need me because I talk to your reader as one of them."

We love the fact that Emily identified a need, filled it, and created a niche that so far, no one else has tried to encroach upon. The important lesson is to look around at your own life. What are you dealing with that you think other people would be interested in learning about or getting help with? The best ideas are often found right in your own backyard.

Roundtable: Working on the Other Side of the Camera

Television can change your life even if you aren't on air. Fashion stylists, makeup artists, and culinary professionals are just a few of the experts who can make the transition to television and work behind the camera. Here are three women who have transformed their careers, broadened their skills, and met amazing people. **Fran Taylor** does wardrobe for the ladies of *The View* and dresses Meredith Vieira on the *Today* show. She has also worked on Barbara Walters's specials and David Letterman's guests. **Julie Clevering**'s makeup wizardry enables the natural beauty of TV stars such as Paula Deen and Giada De Laurentiis come across the small screen. And **Ulli Stachl**, also known as the Food Goddess, is a food stylist who can make hamburger look like filet mignon—if necessary. And she has on *The View, The Rosie O'Donnell Show*, and *The Morning Show with Mike and Juliet*.

Starring You!: *How did each of you get into your business?*

Fran Taylor: I was a buyer for Bergdorf's and Macy's and did not like it. I always wanted to be a dresser and a friend of mine who knew this called me one day and asked me if I wanted to work on *The Charles Perez Show*. I jumped at the chance, and did it happily without an assistant. I knew how to merchandise clothes and put looks together, so that was my start, more than ten years ago.

Ulli Stachl: I was a flight attendant with Pan Am and they went under so I retrained as a chef. I interned with Molly O'Neil at the *New York Times,* helping her with her cookbooks, and it was a lot of fun. A friend of mine worked for Martha Stewart's show and I did some styling for them. Then their executive producer left to start The Women's Supermarket Network with Joan Lunden. The producer saw my résumé, and his wife was a flight attendant, so they hired me. I've done food styling on TV shows ever since. Terence and the other producers on *Rosie* continued to book me on every show they worked on and I continue to get work because of those relationships.

Julie Clevering: A friend of my mom's worked for Estée Lauder and she thought I would be a great makeup artist but I did not want to hear about it. I went to school for fashion design and worked in the restaurant business. My mom's friend contacted me again and told me that Estée Lauder was opening a counter in a Bloomingdale's near my home. Then I started working for Bobbi Brown in Manhattan. That gave me the chance to assist Bobbi on the *Today* show. I loved being the person who helped the talent look good. I also had a dream of living in Hawaii and Bobbi Brown let me run their counter in Hawaii's Neiman Marcus. My first TV experience was a commercial, and I knew then that being on set was my passion. People from around the world would come to the island and shoot commercials, films, and TV segments and I just started assisting in any way I could.

SY: *What aspects of working in TV are special or unique?*
FT: It gives me a forum to show viewers how different women of different ages and shapes can dress beautifully. *The View* is special because it was the first talk show that allowed the hosts to dress casually. Previously everyone had to wear a big red jacket and here is Barbara coming out in jeans and looking great. Women at home see that they can do it too; they learn by example.

US: TV gives me a lot more say in the creativity. If you do food styling for print ads you have the art director and the client telling you what to do. TV styling is very open. The producer, the talent, and I discuss the recipes and the look we want, we break down how the cooking steps should be done, and they leave me to it. I do the logistics, planning, shopping, set up, propping, food beauty, and decorating. I am a one-woman show and it leaves me the creativity.

JC: I learn every single day. Working with Ricki Lake was a magical experience. I learned so much about women and makeup from her. I want to see the woman through her makeup, I do not believe in piling on tons of makeup. Most of the jobs I have been brought in on the producers say we need the talent to look more natural. I discover and use the best products and show women how to look great without having to wear a lot on their faces. Translating that to people through TV is a nice feeling. For example, Giada and Paula look more natural and beautiful now and they wear less makeup.

SY: *What other doors has working in TV opened?*
FT: I have started doing on-air styling—so far on TLC's *A Makeover Story* and *The View.*

US: I am working on three books, one is on food styling for the everyday person; how to make it look appetizing with anecdotes from the shows I have worked on. My next step is to be media trained and start doing on-air work.

JC: I talk at makeup schools, and I have started writing for Paula's magazine, *Cooking with Paula Deen*, dispensing makeup advice, which I love. When I write I have a smile from ear to ear—I have a passion to share what I know.

SY: *Any advice for those who want to work behind the scenes?*
FT: Take any opportunity in TV that you can. I started on a show that lasted a year but that was enough to open the door for me. I have worked in TV ever since.

US: Volunteer. Work as a waitperson at a gala or benefit to get to know people in the industry and talk to the food stylists. Offer your services—it's called "trailing" in the food business and it is a very common way to get started. When you get good enough you will be hired. I recommend people who have worked with me if I cannot be there. Second, be willing. The assistants who are willing to do things and do not turn their noses up at washing dishes are the ones that get the farthest.

JC: Build relationships with people by making them look good. Artists need to embrace this concept. It is about them, not you. This is how I have built long relationships. I met Terence and Marta on *Life & Style,* and I could not imagine what it would be like to work with four women and those girls did not even have a friendship. It was an interesting dynamic and it was not always a smooth situation. I learned how to keep an even mood and make the best of any situation.

A career as a professional expert—that is heady stuff. It's a fantastic way to enhance and supplement your career. We think every person featured in this chapter could have their own show, like Tucker Carlson and Fred Barnes, if they wanted to. And why not? If you have been bitten by the TV bug, why not dream big, wide, and high?

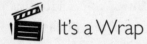 It's a Wrap

- Say yes to all invitations to be on TV. The more you are on the more you become a regular.

- Don't take relationships for granted. Producers move from show to show.

- Keep up on trends and your area of expertise so you always have new information to bring to the table.

- Don't get too comfortable in your role. Constantly reinvent yourself.

- Remember, experts are experts, not producers. No matter how much experience you get, let the producer do his or her job.

Chapter 8

A Host of Options

Television moves at lightning speed. Sell a screenplay and it can sit around for ten years before anything happens—or nothing can happen at all. **You can pitch a show, sell it, and it can be in production and then on within a year.** Plus, in *some* cases, you can make a fortune if your show is a big hit and goes into syndication. Television is nimble and more willing to take chances on unknowns than the film business. For one thing, there is not as much money at stake. There are many revenue streams that can flow from your show as well—live speaking engagements and appearances, broadband distribution, games, text messaging, books, DVDs, magazines, and on and on.

Once you have built a solid reel as an on-air guest or as a paid expert, the next step could be to host a show. With so many cable shows and local original programming, TV executives need people who have new show concepts and/or who can host shows and there are simply not enough professional broadcasters to go around. And often producers want hosts and show ideas from "the field." *Survivor* runner-up Elisabeth Hasselbeck was on *The Rosie O'Donnell Show* and talked about how she loved fashion (and she was a fine arts major at Boston College). Marta spotted her and helped her score the hosting spot on the Style Network's popular show *The Look for Less*.

Here's an assignment: What's your show? Write a description of the kind of show you see yourself hosting or an outline of a show you would like to create. Most show pitches, or treatments, as they are known in the business, are pithy—don't go on too long. A concept pitch should be no longer than one to two paragraphs.

Next, write out a show outline: list the segments, teases, and breaks. Outlines are short too, not more than one page long. Like a segment pitch, it should be a crisp, energetic, precise explanation of your idea. This is a simple format, based on a half-hour, four-segment beauty show we produced:

BEAUTY BEAT

SEGMENT ONE:
"Beauty Babble"—hosts sit around round table to dish about the latest in beauty, gossip, and the always entertaining Hamptons.

- Host intros show and panel: "This is the first and only talk show dedicated to looking and feeling great."
- Relationships that stylists have with their clients—panel will share stories
- Young and Overdone along with Hollywood Smiles—PROPS: photos
- Tried and Tested—Hosts share their favorite product
- Celebrity chat with model BETH OSTROSKY

TEASE (a short promo going to commercial break): **Hamptons Beauty Squad Makeover Next!**

BUMP OUT (extra part of tease): Celeb "Beauty Beat" plug

SEGMENT TWO:
"Hamptons Beauty Squad"—Team beauty hits KMART to look for a resident in desperate need of Hamptons makeover.
TEASE: Hosts visit Hamptons garage sale **"Super Saturday"**
BUMP OUT: Host beauty tip

SEGMENT THREE:
TAPE PIECE: (pretaped segment) **Super Saturday in the Hamptons**
TEASE: *REVEAL MAKEOVER*
BUMP OUT: Beauty fact/tip from one of the hosts/Celebrity drop line

SEGMENT FOUR:
Makeover Reveal—Celebrity makeup artist Kristopher Buckle is pre-set with squad.
Before/after shots. Each expert host tells what they did.

SHOW CLOSE

Even if you are not going to develop your own show, this is still a great exercise. It helps you focus on a concept and develop it in a short, snappy way—that's a useful skill for selling just about any idea to anyone.

After all this time in the business, even we cannot identify a single path to hosting or selling a show. If you are the kind of person who sits back and expects a TV show to come to you, we are not saying it never happens, but your chances are severely limited. So hit the pavement and get creative. You have to be resourceful. There are many ways to get a gig as a host. We have known people who have gotten jobs from going to casting calls advertised on craigslist (especially the New York and Los Angles versions) or on www.cynopsis.com, which provides a free e-mail newsletter that rounds up what's doing in TV and entertainment, including casting calls and open hosting spots. We met with a young woman who moved to New York City from Europe and she got a job hosting a show on the Travel Channel by responding to an ad on *craigslist*. You can also start out as a guest and become a host. David Evangelista started out as a guest and now hosts a show on the TV Guide Channel. Political writers Fred Barnes and Tucker Carlson started out as nonpaid guests too, and both have their own shows.

 I have to tell you …

There are five common ways to get a hosting gig

1. Your TV appearances get you noticed by a casting director, producer, agent, or production company.

2. Someone spots your book or magazine article, thinks it's a concept for a show, tracks you down, and finds you fascinating.

3. You can run into a production executive who finds you fascinating.

4. An agent represents you, and he or she pitches you to host or team you up with one of their production companies.

5. You take your reel and you pitch yourself to a producer, network, or production company you like and admire—and convince them to buy your idea and you.

Marta

For Rachel Ashwell, getting a show was as "simple" as being noticed by Marta and her team at the Style Network. She visited Rachel's Los Angeles Shabby Chic store, fell in love with what she saw, and signed her for a series of shows by the same name. It helped that she also had three books out, with the promise of more. They helped her clout and credibility. "There is nothing like TV for brand awareness. I am still stopped in the street, and people tell me they love the show, even though it's not being made anymore. It is being shown somewhere in the world all the time," she says.

We want to make one thing clear right away, however. If your aim in becoming a host or creating a show is to make money, put on the brakes. If it was easy, we would all be millionaires or living on easy street, and we're not. Some people host shows for little or no money, as a way of building brand recognition—and in that sense it's worth the effort.

Cable is known for not paying talent particularly well. Some companies pay more than others; one well-known woman's network pays talent about seven thousand dollars per episode. Some cable networks pay less. It all depends on how well funded the network is, how much experience the talent has, and how established his or her name is. Much of the money in television comes from syndication and after proving yourself with viewers. A noncelebrity host of a syndicated talk show could make from $150,000 to $250,000 per season. A host on a cable show can range from $5,000 to $10,000 per episode, and a bit more if they have a lot of experience. Some cable networks "buy" the person for a year with an annual contract, and might pay them $50,000 to $75,000 for beginners. And, of course, after your first year, there is a correlation between ratings and salary—the higher your ratings, the fatter your paycheck.

Get on TV because you love it, because it enhances your life and your brand, not because you think the road is paved with gold. It's paved with hard knocks, lots of work, and creativity, energy, and fun. What follows are some of the ways you can help make your own "starring you" moment a reality. Keep in mind that a show starts with *you—your* talent, *your* knowledge, *your* enthusiasm, and *your* stick-to-it-iveness.

The Agent in Your Toolbox

If you think of yourself as talent, an agent can arrange auditions, get you meetings with casting directors, and negotiate deals for you. If you are an expert with an idea for a show, a TV agent can pitch the idea to the right development people, put a "package" together with other clients, and negotiate a deal. Managers also help you get in to see the right people. We, for example, introduce talent to production companies, get them placement in magazines and segment TV, develop their clout and brand awareness, and then help them establish relationships with agents and move to the next level.

Keep in mind that the Hollywood glamour of being with an agency doesn't mean you can leave your career in their hands. A lot of agents have hundreds of clients, and the tendency for the client is to sit back and think, Oh, I have an agent and a PR person so I will just wait around until they bring me my stardom on a platter. Terence was with one of the big three as a producer and they got him maybe two interviews the entire time. He still got all his own jobs. **No one cheerleads for you like you can.** You are your own best salesperson, even if you have a great team that includes an agent or a manager.

Meet and "interview" prospective agents (they are interviewing you so you might as well interview them). Sometimes people at big agencies have never met people they represent. We were casting for a reporter on a talk show and we had narrowed it down to a couple of candidates, one of which we had seen only on a tape. A couple of days before we were going to shoot, Terence thought we should bring the guy in because we had not seen him in person. He was much too short for the part. We have absolutely nothing against short people, but he was completely wrong for the job. Our point is that you have to be careful that you are being represented in the best and most honest way. The agent never took the time to meet with this person and if he had he would have realized the person was wrong for certain jobs, including ours. Make sure the agent knows who you are; it's the only way they can pitch you effectively. You want the agent to be a fan of yours and motivated to help you. Talent have told us, "My agent is doing the work," and we think, Uh, some of them aren't. Otherwise cable shows would not use *craigslist* to look for talent.

Smaller agencies may have the advantage of offering personal attention. Mark Turner at Abrams Artists Agency in New York City says, "We are not the biggest agency, so you will not get lost in the shuffle of big celebrities. Every e-mail and phone call gets returned, and we are proactive, not reactive like some of the bigger agencies."

Mark specializes in therapy, self-help, relationships, lifestyle, and interior design hosts. The majority of his clients are not household names, but they do host or anchor both national and local shows. Client Norma Vally, for example, hosts *Toolbelt Diva* on the Discovery Home Channel and appeared on that network's *Rally Round the House*. Arlene Tur hosts shows on the Travel Channel and Molly Pesce has hosted shows on networks ranging from Animal Planet to Comedy Central. "I am constantly pitching and bringing them to the attention of producers and development people. They could do it themselves, but they will not be taken as seriously," he says.

When hiring an agency, whether it's a big house or a boutique firm, find out what access they have to TV decision makers. Are they one of the first five firms or agents producers call when they are looking for talent? Check out their client list. Who is on it? What shows have they been able to cast talent in? Have they packaged any TV shows? The reality is a great idea is a great idea and a great talent is a great talent but you can increase your chances with an agent. An agent is a *tool,* not the whole answer.

Joanna Jordan, a talent booker, says a good way to select representation is to get on the same team as the person you compare yourself to. "If you want to be the next Simon Cow-

---

 I have to tell you ...

Not everyone was meant to have his or her own show

Just because you might be good at plastic surgery doesn't mean you should be on Discovery hosting a show about it. But that does not mean you cannot develop a show—figure out whether you are a host or a show creator. Some people can be both, but if you are not comfortable in front of the camera, consider developing a show and selling it, and then letting someone else act as the host. It's like being the CEO of your company and being smart enough to realize the spokesperson may not be you.

Marta

ell, try to get a meeting with his agents. If you want to be the next *American Chopper* guy, find out who reps him."

Powerhouse Packager: Mark Itkin

Most agents look at unsolicited reels and résumés. It may take them some time to get back to you, but most of the pros we know eventually look at everything they get because they are in the business of finding new talent. And like producers, they also watch a lot of TV in hopes of spotting untapped talent. Mark Itkin, executive vice president and worldwide head of syndication, cable, and nonfiction programming for the William Morris Agency in Los Angeles (one of the top three agencies in the country), has packaged such network, cable, and syndication projects as *Big Brother, Fear Factor, Buffy the Vampire Slayer,* and *WWE SmackDown,* among many others. Despite the fact that he probably knows everyone worth knowing in Hollywood, he still reads popular magazines and watches TV to scout for talent.

Interesting stories and unique situations catch Mark's eye the most. "I was watching the *Today* show and saw Jeff Baxter. He played with Steely Dan and the Doobie Brothers. But now he goes by the nickname Skunk and is one of the national-security world's most well known counterterrorism experts, although he still jams. I thought, What a great candidate to base a scripted series on. It could not be a reality show because a lot of what he does is secret. So now I am working with him to develop a fictional show based on his life."

Mark also discovered a woman who was part of Women of Faith, a nondenominational Christian women's organization that holds large women's weekends in various locations.

Twenty thousand women come together for three days and listen to motivational speakers, among other events—that's a large built-in audience. Mark makes sure he knows what is going on at venues like that. He discovered Nicole Johnson—author, comedian, and singer—at one such Women of Faith event.

"She has a spiritual message; if you were not in that world you would not know about her, but I thought she could do something interesting for daytime TV. We are meeting producers and syndicates to build a show because her message is broader than the niche she is in. She is beautiful but not intimidating, and her message is universal enough to go mainstream, but she needed an agent to take her there," says Mark. **"If someone is in a niche business, is doing well, and wants to go mainstream that is a good time to get an agent."**

A family of pediatricians including a father and three sons, and a mother who is a nurse, captured Mark's imagination recently. "The father is Bill Sears. He has done guest appearances on *Dr. Phil,* PBS, and the Discovery Health Channel, but the whole family is involved. A manager brought the family to me and said, I think it is time for these people to go to the next step," he says. The challenge for Mark was to figure out how to take a very unique situation. "I thought, Let me introduce the entire family to Phil McGraw. We are working on spinning a daily reality show out of his show."

Just knowing someone like Mark might be watching you on TV is heady stuff for anyone to contemplate. That said, less than 5 percent of the people Mark sees end up being represented by him (which does not mean they do not find another terrific agent). "I meet people, get referrals, letters, and packages all day long." He cautions that he does not look at any show idea without having its source sign a property release. "It relieves us of liability—I cannot and will not look at any unsolicited idea without that. I try to look at everything, but it's difficult." Mark says you may have better luck with a younger, hungry agent if you are just starting out. "In 1985 a guy cold-called me with an idea for a game show called *Wordplay*. Today I would not see that person but at that time I was searching for clients. I put it together with one of my packaging clients [a production company or a producer that sells shows], and we sold it," he says.

Finally, Mark advises would-be show hosts or creators to stay realistic and flexible. "You may think you are the best singer or have the best TV idea in the world, and if you believe that you should pursue your dreams. **But when you start shopping it and experienced people give you constructive notes, remain open-minded.** Don't argue. Even if they are wrong, they may cause you to rethink and improve your approach."

Talent Booker: Joanna Jordan

Joanna Jordan, former late-night show booker and now owner of her own company, Central Talent Booking, makes it her business, literally, to look for show-worthy personalities. Talent bookers can also help you get guest appearances and hosting gigs. Unlike agents, who generally earn a 10 percent commission on jobs they secure for you and negotiate on your behalf, the company who needs the talent pays the booker. Getting on a booker's radar screen is not easy because theirs is a business-to-business profession, not easily infiltrated by the man (or woman) on the street.

Joanna is hired by television shows, magazines, radio stations, and cable networks to act as their talent department. While she focuses on finding guest talent for shows (in turn, a great way to get noticed by development execs), she does meet people she thinks could support a show. She works with everyone from comedians to musical talent to regular people with interesting stories to tell or messages to share. Getting to her or someone like her usually requires the help of an agent or PR person.

"We do a lot of meet and greets, which is when people come in with their PR rep. I always want a tape and a photograph so I get a sense of how they look. We often have them come by the office and chat with them. I cannot book someone who cannot finish a sentence. People need to understand that the clock is ticking. Arnold Schwarzenegger is brilliant at that. He decides what he is going to say about the movie and himself and whatever questions were asked he would reply with the same answers with the message that he wanted to get out. Every now and again you meet somebody who could carry a show. Since we are talking to people at the cable networks like Animal Planet, Comedy Central, and TLC all the time, we can say to them, 'This guy should have a TV show,' and we have done that," she says.

Joanna's eye for talent has been honed by working with a lot of celebrities on late-night television. "When you meet fifteen famous people a week, and feel their level of energy and freshness, you can identify that star quality in nonfamous people." She finds a lot of good people by watching the morning shows. They have so many segments to fill that you do see guests who could turn into something more, especially if their expertise is appealing to a cable niche such as health, travel, animals, or lifestyle. "We track them down, I get the tape and a picture, backup from an article, and shoot off an e-mail to someone I know at TLC and then we set it up and have their casting person check them out."

For people with comedic and theatrical ambitions, Joanna says a booking on a talk show really opens doors for starring roles. "I had a conversation with a friend who did a one-woman show in a comedy club, who wants to be a sitcom star. I told her to get a friend to tape the show, and edit it down to the best seven minutes, and send it to the stand-up bookers at late-night shows. That opened immediate doors for her because it was tangible proof of her abilities."

The right TV appearances can catapult a little-known actor or personality to stardom. When Bill Cosby subbed for David Letterman when he was recovering from surgery, the comedian asked Joanna to book a fun, super-sexy girl. "I had met Latin actress Sofía Vergara for lunch with her rep in New York. She completely blew me away with her fantastic personality. Every guy in the kitchen was trying to get her autograph because she was known in the Latin market. I thought she had great potential to become a host, actress, or movie star. So I said to Bill, I know just the girl. He kept her on for sixteen minutes, and she used that tape to get a series called *The Knights of Prosperity*, about a group of friends who set out to rob celebrities. When I saw her she was very upfront and said, 'You are the reason I am on TV now.' She could have easily turned down the booking and said, No, I will wait for Letterman to come back. But she seized the moment," says Joanna.

Round 'Em Up: VH1

As Joanna says, sometimes a well-timed appearance or a well-edited tape of you being charming and witty is all it takes to open the right door—to a development executive or a show runner. There are so many showcases for talent on TV, from reality shows, which we discussed in chapter one, to appearances on segment TV. Getting a gig on a cable network that features a variety of talent in various show formats is another way to start hosting and to build toward bigger shows. VH1 and the Discovery networks are two such outlets. They both provide numerous opportunities for hosting. Doing these roundup shows pays nothing, but a lot of people do it for the exposure. "I do them to keep my face out there," says style maven David Evangelista.

Some of the most coveted "casting calls" in the business are for VH1's roundup shows, such as the *I Love the* . . . series and *Best Week Ever*. All sorts of not-quite-famous comedians, experts, and journalists strut their humor and entertaining commentary on these shows, including rocker turned counterterrorism expert Jeff Baxter, who agent Mark Itkin is working with to develop a scripted show; stylist expert David Evangelista; Mo Rocca, comedian and political satirist; and singer/songwriter Lisa Loeb.

"A spot on a VH1 show is so helpful for someone's reels, for talking to agents or development people. When they see that on a résumé it gives them credibility, especially if it's someone who is trying to get acting work because it demonstrates that they are smart, funny, and potentially right for a part," says Jim Kozloff, VH1's director of casting & talent development, who often sits in a room all day observing general casting sessions and listening to people share their thoughts on Britney Spears or Pop Rocks candy, in hopes that more than one of them will be right for a VH1 roundup show. He's got to have one of the best jobs in TV.

"The *I Love the* . . . shows has some money behind it so we can spend a little more on talent. We are looking for people who are recognizable and funny, with interesting faces. They should be established, even if they aren't household names," says Jim. That means the person could be a supporting character in a sitcom, or he or she has a comedic background. *Best Week Ever,* which is shown every Friday, has a smaller production budget, and features up-and-coming comedians and journalists. "The final tier of talent are anonymous talking heads during the day, which we use when we are using video clips, talking about celebrities with bad hair and red carpet fashions. Those people come from the grassroots comedy world, and it's a good way to find out if they can deliver on another level," says Jim. Even then, Jim says they have to walk a fine line between witty and mean. "A lot of stand-up comedians don't work out because they go for the jugular," he cautions.

Some VH1 shows lend themselves to editorial and expert types. "We did an hour on plastic surgery and we did not make fun of people. We wanted to be more serious, so we used a lot of editorial people and experts rather than using funny people. We can do that because we produce everything in-house, so we're very flexible and our producers are very creative," he says. Whitney Matheson, the *USA Today* columnist, is one of Jim's favorite scribes. "I love reading Whitney's column and she came by to say hello, but she was tentative about being on camera. But she is very funny and cute," he says.

For columnists and others not on Jim's radar, talent comes to him via managers and agents. "We also do a lot of scouting in the comedy world." The unifying factor for all VH1 personalities is that they love, understand, and are knowledgeable about popular culture. "I test candidates on their pop culture awareness. We don't need people who can read a script, because we expect the talent to come up with their own material, to ad lib, and to think fast on their feet." He relates the story of meeting a former *Apprentice* contestant who was being pushed by her management. He met with the woman, who was attractive, but she didn't watch TV. She expected to be provided with research, but VH1 doesn't have time for that. "We ask people to be themselves so it has to be inherent in them to be enthusiastic about the topic," says Jim. She didn't get the gig.

Even if being on a VH1 roundup show is not your dream (and we can't imagine why it wouldn't be), Jim's point about having a quick and intelligent wit is a good one. All casting directors want that quality in a host. We understand that wit and charm are natural attributes, and difficult to learn if you are without a sense of humor. That's why all actors are not natural hosts or "good interviews"—they can act but they have trouble being themselves. Do your friends think you're funny? Do you find it easy to make wry observations about the foibles and fumbles of celebrities and politicians? We go back to the question reality producer Denise Cramsey asked in the first chapter: Do people notice you when you walk into a room? If you answer yes to those questions, you may be on your way to being a great host.

Discover Your Cast Calling

One talent pro who looks for those qualities is Todd Miller, the director of talent development and casting at Discovery Communications, Inc. He does casting for specific network shows and oversees casting when he can't do it himself. "I am a one-man band. We have so many networks (Animal Planet, the

Travel Channel, Discovery, Discovery Home, FitTV to name a few) so I meet people not always for a specific show, but to see if they have something to bring to the network. Sometimes our development department develops a show without talent attached and then our paths cross," says Todd.

For Todd, scouting for hosts and experts means dealing with agents and managers on a daily basis, since more and more host hopefuls have representation. "We have a good relationship with that community. We also reach out to the reality and theatrical communities." The caveat? They have to be willing to work nonunion because Discovery is nonunion. It's usually not a problem.

"Web site postings or contacting specific organizations helps us find experts. For example, I have to find chefs with a healthy bent so I contacted the Natural Gourmet Institute and talked to their placement department about potential staff members who might be appropriate," says Todd. "It's all about spreading the word and talking to people and organizations. Depending on what we are looking for I can do a Google search and come up with people. And I have done casting off of craigslist. We found Cathy Riva for our show *Party Girl* from craigslist." And you thought we were kidding when we told you talent scouts use craigslist!

Although the kind of person he looks for depends on the show or network involved, Todd does look for certain universal qualities in show talent. "A very natural conversational ability, ad lib and interpersonal interaction skills are essential. It is not about being able to read a teleprompter," he says. Discovery hosts have to be comfortable in their own skin, says Todd, who defines a person with host potential as witty and charming, and not too newsy or plastic. "We don't need people who are dressed to the nines in pearls or stuck in the old-school style of very stiff hosting. Experts need camera presence, but if they have the body of knowledge we need, we can help them pull off what we need them to do."

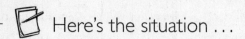

Here's the situation . . .

Go back to the "know the shows" rule if you are pitching yourself as a host or pitching a show

It drives me crazy to meet with people who have no idea what my studio or network does. If you are meeting with a major studio, know what shows they do. Every major studio has a Web site that says what's on, and it's usually broken down by category. Find out if they outsource their shows as well. Some networks produce their own shows, others source them out to production companies, and still others do a combination of the two. Watch what production companies are doing a show that is similar to yours and pitch them your idea or talent.

Terence

Developing Women: Alex Duda and Roni Selig

When you have an agent, a reel of appearances, and a show idea, the people who can make it happen are people like Alex Duda and Roni Selig. Roni is currently senior vice president of current programming and East Coast development at Buena Vista Productions (the syndication division of Walt Disney). Buena Vista is responsible for hits such as *Live with Regis and Kelly* and *The View*.

Alex is now the executive producer for *The Tyra Banks Show*, and was the executive producer and creator of *Elimidate* and *E! Fashion Emergency*, executive producer of *Talk Soup*, and has produced hundreds of specials for E! Entertainment Television and the TV Guide Channel. But we've been working with Alex for years, Marta at E! and Terence at *Elimidate*. Roni was executive producer at *The Rosie O'Donnell Show* (Terence was one of her producers), an executive producer at Oxygen, and helped codevelop *The View*.

A "passion to communicate" is how Alex describes a compelling host. "So often the best hosts and show ideas come from people from a field other than television who have a passion," she says. She points to grandmother and "sexpert" Sue Johanson as a surprisingly great host—unexpected because she does not fit the stereotype of the thirty-something, polished, fashionable, hip person who would be far more predictable in such a role.

"Rachael Ray is another perfect example. She got a network show by first developing a following on the Food Network that went beyond just food. Very often people can parlay a career in a niche market into a general one if they have the ability to communicate effectively and garner a demographically broad fan base," she says. You see someone like Rachael and think it happens overnight, but she has been working at it for years—she started locally in upstate New York, not exactly a huge media market. But she stuck with it, just like all successful TV people.

"If we found a person who we thought has host potential, we would try them out in a segment or we would create a sizzle clip as a sales tape," says Alex. It's not a big investment of money, but just enough to let the network know what they are getting. Booking multiple segments on a variety of shows is another way a producer like Alex can gauge audience reaction. "From that perspective you try to get on as many shows as you can so a producer can see something substantial," says Alex.

Passion combined with a good idea is only halfway down the road to selling a show. "Identify the production companies that do the kind of show you want to do," says Alex, "and try to get a meeting with them. An agent helps because they can open the door, or you can try to go to the network directly." If network development people have seen you on cable shows, or the cable networks have seen you on segment TV, there may be interest and buzz about you, and development people will be interested in hearing about your concept. Getting in to a large organization like that can be more difficult if you are an unknown or little known. There are also many independent production companies that sell to both cable and major networks, and it could be easier to get a meeting with them. However, even small production companies don't usually accept unsolicited ideas—an agent is still your best bet to getting past the receptionist.

"**Make connections any way you can**," says Alex. "People want to work with people they know and trust, so cold calling is tough. But anyone who can vouch for you or make an introduction, even an assistant, gives you an edge. Think about all the people you know—it's the six degrees of separation principle. Ask around—you will be surprised how connected you are."

Production companies make pilots (a sample episode) that they then use to sell a series to a network. "If you are an individual without the time or resources to shoot a pilot, and the concept is hot, you can take your reel to a meeting with a production company or network, and then explain the idea in a verbal pitch," says Alex. "If you have a little money, it's a good idea to shoot at least a segment or scene from the show." That's one reason that it's a good idea to partner with a production company. Once you are in business with a production company, you need to have a lawyer to structure your deal.

Buena Vista's Roni Selig says the qualities of a great host are "**personality, poise, intellect, a sense of humor, and performance that converge to create lightning in a bottle.**" That's just the beginning, of course. Roni, like Alex, says you have to develop a following with audiences on as many segments as you can in order to break out from the pack and become a host. If you don't have what it takes to command a show on your own, there is a way around it, says Roni. "You can also combine your skills and work in an ensemble. That's what made *The View* successful. [Former cast member] Star tried to have her own show (*Jones & Jury*). Joy Behar adds 'the funny' to the show, but the chance of her getting a show on her own would have been difficult," she says.

The question development executives like Roni are always asking themselves (and it's a question you have to ask yourself as well) is what magic is the potential host adding to the viewer's life? "It's got to be something you cannot get elsewhere that is so yummy and so reliably compelling that the host becomes a friend. **If you cannot become a companion to the viewer you will not make it more than two years,**" she says.

If you have developed a following on segment TV and believe you have something special, an agency has an incredible amount of power to knock on doors and get you in front of the big syndication companies and arrange a development deal. "That is the first step. Next comes a pilot and if it tests well, you have to pitch it like the greatest salesperson in the world," explains Roni, who says the passion for the idea and the idea itself are of equal weight. "No one has the exact formula, otherwise all shows would be hits, so that means there is a ton of doubt so if you can eliminate doubt in your pitch it gets you closer to your deal," she says. That means making your pitch bulletproof to convince the doubters that it will work.

The best presentations are written proposals or in-person pitches. "There are pros and cons to putting something on tape. If it does not fly it's dead from the get-go. Better to make the verbal pitch and sell it with your heart and sole and passion," says Roni. Remember that development execs are busy and they will give you literally five minutes to make the pitch. They know in that amount of time if they want to pursue the conversation. "If the personality is there, the pitch will go longer because the development person is trying to ascertain if they have the layers and range of talent needed to be in front of the camera," she says.

How do you know that a development team wants to bite? According to Roni, "You can tell by the questions they ask, including the projected budget. That's a clear indication that there may be interest because they are thinking, If we were to produce this how much will it cost?" Then there are people who have complete game faces—and you have no idea what they are thinking. So be prepared. "It's frustrating, but you have to walk away and hope they like it. Showing enthusiasm means dollar signs to them, so often development people play it close to the vest because they do not want to make a huge investment in an unknown."

☆ Anatomy of a Food Show: Paula Deen

Paula Deen is one of the most compelling stories in television. She defies the stereotypes we are all told you need to fit in order to be successful on TV—being young, skinny, and terminally hip. Paula proves there is not one accepted route, complete with handlers, managers, lawyers, and agents. She had none of those things when she was discovered. And like so many of the people we have featured in this book, from designer Rachel Ashwell to lawyer Joe Tacopina, she got to where she is because she was really good at what she did, her personality sparkles naturally, and she has a passion for her topic, in this case good old-fashioned southern cooking. Her story is educational—it's really the perfect TV story.

"When I had The Bag Lady (a small business of prepared brown bag lunches for business people) I could not have gotten into a newspaper let alone on TV," says Paula, talking about her early days as a single mom struggling to find a way to raise her two young sons and earn a living. "Then I took over a restaurant in the Best Western Hotel in Savannah. Those years were the hardest years of my life, but once I opened the Lady and Sons downtown it made me very visible to tourists and locals," she says.

Then, of course, fate intervened, which is totally unpredictable—but being in the right place at the right time can sort of be controlled by picking the right location for your business. "Not too long after I relocated, Clint Eastwood started filming *Midnight in the Garden of Good and Evil*, which was based on the book of the same name, published by Random House," she says. One of the book's editors was walking down Congress Street while it was raining so she ducked inside Paula's restaurant. "She was surprised to get this wonderful meal," says Paula, and "apparently she went back to New York and a few days later she called me up and asked me if I wanted to do a cookbook."

"I had a self-published cookbook, which I sent the editor, and three or four days later the editor called back and said they wanted to publish it," says Paula, still sounding amazed at her good fortune. "I pretended to know what they were talking about but later I asked my son who and what Random House was." Paula worked on the revision for a year, and then told her editor she wanted to sell it on QVC. She was familiar with QVC and saw the way they sold the products. It was a great marketing tool. "I cannot tell you what it meant to go on QVC and get that national exposure. People related and trusted me," she says. That was only the beginning of her love affair with the tube (or its love affair with her).

Several years later, fate intervened again. Paula met a woman who had moved to Savannah from New York. "She was a former Victoria's Secret model, and we became good speaking friends. I would talk to her while she ate and she said she had a friend she wanted me to meet—Gordon Elliott." Sure enough, the next week Gordon came and featured Paula on his show *Gordon's Door Knob Dinner*. "We hit it off famously, we laughed and laughed and had the best time because we have the same sense of humor. He asked if I would do a couple of guest shots on his show, and my show came about from there," says Paula. Not so fast, though: it took Gordon and Paula, who now had an agent, two years to convince the Food Network that she was a sellable brand, and *Paula's Home Cooking* was born. "I just don't give up," she says.

Paula's advice to TV stars in the making is to stick to what you do best. In her case, it's simple, yummy, home cooking. "It is great to watch a certified chef cook, it's for entertainment; it does not mean you'll try to cook what they are making. My show is very attainable. I assume that the viewer has never made a sandwich, so I make demonstrations clear and precise," she says. Physical location is also an important component to Paula's show and to her brand. "I cannot be in a studio setting; it has to be a home kitchen setting. That's an important part of who I am and what I convey to the audience."

Finally, Paula says stamina is important if you want to be a TV cook. "I think I'm a good cook, but no better than a lot of other women. My best asset is that I can stand longer than the person next to me."

Paula's latest show, *Paula's Party,* has an audience. The production company created a couple of specials first, to test the market for a show with an audience, and it worked. Paula is a gracious host, and her audience participants don't seem contrived like they do on some other lifestyle shows with audiences. She genuinely likes her fans.

Cordelia Bowe, Paula's executive producer, says the show has a staff of two producers and a small key group of others who brainstorm ideas and figure out what the theme of the segments will be. "We get endless submissions from her Web site, many recipes accompanied by interesting stories, and some of those people will be pulled to be on a segment. A typical day of preproduction includes coming up with show concepts and individual segment concepts, and deciding which ones will be shot in the field and which ones will take place in the studio." They are usually also in postproduction on shows already shot, which means they are in the editing room being cut and tweaked. Plus, Paula's original show is still in production—she's doing a lot of standing!

The Trooper

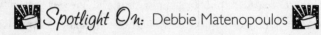 *Spotlight On:* Debbie Matenopoulos

Whether or not you become the host or star of your own show, disappointment and rejection are part of the game. Remember in chapter one, when Marta says this business can be one of nos? It's true, even for people who seem to be on top of the world. Things change in an instant—one minute you're the darling of the airwaves and the next minute you are a has-been—sometimes even before you were a "been." The good news is that TV is forgiving.

Debbie Matenopoulos is someone who was placed in a high-profile position—the youngest cohost of *The View*—only to be fired and rejected and resurrected because of her own tenacity and guts. No matter what business you're in, or whether you want to be on TV or not, Debbie's story is enlightening, inspiring, and a ringing endorsement of the adage "success is the best revenge." After all, she was asked back on *The View* not that long ago. Talk about what goes around!

Terence has known Debbie since her *View* days, and says she is a reminder to us all to *never* give up your dreams, no matter what. It's a cliché, but it's true. No one who has ever had any success in anything has ever gotten there by rolling over and playing dead. They kept going no matter how many doors closed, and no matter what other people said.

Starring You!: *How did you start?*

Debbie Matenopoulos: I was only twenty-one, and a production assistant at MTV. I did not know who I was. I was going to NYU and all of a sudden I was sitting next to Barbara Walters. That in itself was a unique experience—it was singular. No one will have that experience again; I was the youngest person to be on daytime TV. It was sink or swim.

SY: *How did that come about?*

DM: I knew no one. I met a casting director at a party. I had pink hair at the time so it wasn't like I was trying to be on network TV. My aspiration was to be a VJ. But this casting director was taken with me and he became friends with my roommate and he called her and asked if I would like to audition for Barbara. So I went to ABC and did it. I beat out seven hundred other girls by showing up at the audition with a bowling bag as a purse and a *Welcome Back, Kotter* T-shirt and being honest. That's why they hired me and fired me.

SY: *What was that like?*

DM: Things are still painful—to everyone reading this book, know that you will be fired or not asked back *at least once* if not more times. I did not have a skill set for being a host. The light would come on and I had to tap dance and hope that the audience would be forgiving. I learned by doing. The first day I threw up. I made a million and a half mistakes on *live* TV in front of the *world*.

SY: *So I guess it was a learning experience.*

DM: The most important thing I learned was always be true and honest. Those are the two things that connect people at home. No matter how bad I messed up or how stupid the shit that came out of my twenty-one-year-old mouth was—they really should have given me a smaller part—it was authentic. The advertisers would not care if I had been doing the same things on MTV. But *The View*? They were not ready for that. Sincerity endeared me to the fans. When they got rid of me the fans did a huge "Bring Back Debbie" campaign. After being beaten down I did not think I was so great. But I learned that there is a difference between rough around the edges and too polished.

SY: *So how do you survive public humiliation, especially when it's really not your fault?*

DM: Having the skill set to do it well is important. Having the faith in yourself and being comfortable in your skin, allowing the audience to see your flaws. I call it television with hiccups or television that burps because at any moment I will do something that is not the proper way to do something—when I am speaking I may say it in a downtown hip way. Maybe it is not what every American wants to hear but they may say it's interesting she is comfortable enough to do that. I never cut when I blow a word—it is far better to cough and say excuse me and continue. I hate TV that is so polished and canned—that's not life.

SY: *How do you keep going?*

DM: If you really believe in your product, whether it is your book, you, a skin-care line, or whatever, I do not care who rejects you. Continue down the path. This business is 99.9 percent rejection even when you are on top. Now I have three jobs: I have a show on E! Entertainment Television and I sold a movie to Oxygen that I wrote and that I will be in. It does not matter. I still go in for auditions. If you believe you are the right person you better follow up—let them know. I go back to my agent—I say I do not think the other person is better, I write the producers or director a letter, whatever it takes to get the decision maker to hear me out. Maybe they won't change their mind but they will respect how much I believe in the project or myself. Everyone relates to that.

If that doesn't work, pick yourself up and keep on going. The business is about surviving; it's not the most talented or best liked. If you look at peoples' careers and their highs and lows it is about people who stuck it out and refused to say no—this person may not like me or this network might like me. You cannot please everyone—it's a cliché because it is true. You are never going to have 100 percent of the vote. Find a place that does want you. Hone your skills. Then you can go back to the people who said you were not good enough, and then have them beg you to join them because you *are* good enough.

What's Next: The New Media

As technology progresses, we will get entertainment and information in new ways. Everyone in the business is thinking in terms of multiple platforms now, whether it is streaming video, text messaging, or iPod webcasts. "I think about multiple platforms with every show I package now," says William Morris agent Mark Itkin. "You need the additional revenue from those platforms to make money, because it's hard for the client to control and own show rights." They *can* make money from ancillary products. While the new media platforms do not represent substantial revenue streams yet, they will eventually, especially as young demographics familiar with the latest technology age and become coveted consumers. According to Mark, "To stream a show online so a potential audience can see it before it airs means the potential for a show becomes much bigger."

Jane Buckingham, president of The Intelligence Group (www.youthintelligence.com), a trend tracking firm, and the host and author of the show and book *The Modern Girl's Guide to Life,* says the evolution of new media brings more opportunities for talent as well. "We see it on YouTube (www. youtube.com) and podcasts. There are all kinds of opportunities for new voices to be heard and new talents to emerge. There is more opportunity for the people to choose what they like versus the industry choosing what we should see," says Jane. Having said that, Jane predicts it may become harder for people to have sustainable and long careers because audiences will have so many choices and options—and shorter attention spans.

The constant inundation of new material and people makes

it all the more important to have a clear brand, position, and differentiating points. Talent must be clear as to whom they are and what they have to offer. To that end, our next *Starring You!* venture enters into the new media landscape.

 It's a Wrap

- Search Web sites such as craigslist, entertainmentcareer.net, www.varietycareers.com, cynopsis.com, or www.Mandy.com for casting calls. Many hosts get their jobs this way.

- Personality, poise, intellect, a sense of humor, and performance are the ingredients necessary to be a screen-shattering host.

- Find an agent who sincerely believes in your brand and message.

- Never rest on your laurels just because you have people working for you—you are still your own best PR person.

- Never give up—persistence pays off. One day you're in, the next you're out, and then you're back in!

Wrap Party—Are You Ready to Be a Star?

We've come to the end, which is really just the beginning for you. You've finished the book and completed all our assignments. You are now ready for your *Starring You!* moment. It's time to call the local news and pitch them your story; try to get your cookbook published; or run for president of the PTA. Opportunities to improve your life using the *Starring You!* techniques are endless.

The key is to be persistent, to believe in yourself and your dream, to knock on every door. Be on the lookout, because you never know where your next opportunity is going to come from. Getting this book made is a great example of these principles. If we could make this happen, you can catch your star too. We followed through and believed in our message. When people said, "You will never have a book," we did not listen. We found the right team, we did the work, and guess what: you're going to see our faces in bookstores across America, and on TV!

You can sit back and watch TV or you can get up off the

couch and be a star. As we said in the beginning, we want to hear from you—share your experiences, including what worked, by logging on to our Web site at www.starring–you. com and letting us know.

Stay tuned and thanks for watching!

RESOURCES

Television & Cable Networks

A & E / Arts and Entertainment
235 East 45th Street, New York, NY 10017
212-210-1340 / F: 212-850-9304 www.aande.com

ABC—New York
7 West 66th Street, 9th Floor New York, NY 10023
212-456-7777 http://abc.go.com

ABC—California
500 South Buena Vista Street, Burbank, CA 91521
818-460-7477 http://abc.go.com

ABC—Family
10960 Wilshire Boulevard, Los Angeles, CA 90024
212-456-7777 www.abcfamily.go.com

ABC—News
7 West 66th Street, New York, NY 10023
212-456-7777 www.abcnews.go.com

Altitude Sports and Entertainment
1000 Chopper Circle, Denver, CO 80204
303-405-1100 www.altitude.tv

AMC / American Movie Classics
200 Jericho Quadrangle, Jericho, NY 11753
516-396-3000 www.amctv.com

The America Channel
120 International Parkway, Suite 220 Heathrow, FL 32746
407-333-3031 www.americachannel.us

America One Network
6125 Airport Freeway, Suite 100 Haltom City, TX 76117
817-546-1400 www.americaone.com

American Life TV Network
650 Massachusetts Avenue, Washington, D.C. 20001
202-289-6633 www.goodtv.com

Animal Planet
7700 Wisconsin Avenue, Bethesda, MD 20814
301-986-1999 www.animal.discovery.com

BBC America
7475 Wisconsin Avenue, Suite 1100 Bethesda, MD 20814
301-347-2222 www.bbcamerica.com

BET / Black Entertainment Television
1235 W Street, NE Washington, D.C. 20018
202-608-2000 www.bet.com

The Biography Channel
235 East 45th Street, New York, NY 10017
212-210-1340 www.biographychannel.com

Black Belt TV
P.O. Box 3215, San Dimas, CA 91773
909-971-9300 www.blackbelttv.com

Bloomberg TV
499 Park Avenue, New York, NY 10022
212-318-2000 www.bloomberg.com/tv

BNN / Boston Neighborhood Network
8 Park Plaza, Suite 2240, Boston, MA 02116
617-720-3781/ F: 617-720-3781 www.bnntv.org

Bravo
2 Park Avenue,11th Floor, New York, NY 10016
212-561-1000 www.bravotv.com

Buena Vista Television
500 South Buena Vista, Burbank, CA 91521
818-560-1000 http://bventertainment.go.com

Cartoon Network
1050 Techwood Drive, NW Atlanta, GA 30318
404-885-4390 www.catoonnetwork.com

CBS
51 West 52nd Street, New York, NY 10019
212-975-3247 www.cbs.com

CBS Paramount (Network, Domestic & Int'l)
524 West 57th Street, New York, NY 10019
212-975-3247 www.cbsnews.com

Channel One
6203 B. Variel Avenue, Woodland Hills, CA 91367
818-226-6200 www.channelone.com

CBN / Christian Broadcast Network
977 Centerville Turnpike, Virginia Beach, VA 23463
757-226-7000 www.cbn.com

The Church Channel
2442 Michelle, Tustin, CA 92780
714-832-2950 www.churchchannel.org

Cine Latino
Boulevard Puerto Adreo 486 Col., Moctezuma, Mexico, D.F.
+ 52 (0)55 5764 8211

Cinemax
1100 Avenue of the Americas, New York, NY 10036
212-512-1000 www.cinemax.com

Classic Sports Network / ESPN Classics
ESPN Plaza, Bristol, CT 06010
860-766-2000 http://sports.espn.go.com/espn/classic/index

CMT / Country Music Television
2806 Opryland Drive, Nashville, TN 37214
615-335-8350 www.cmt.com

CNBC
900 Sylvan Avenue, Engelwood Cliffs, NJ 07632
877-251-5685 www.cnbc.com

C-NET Network
235 Second Street, San Francisco, CA 94105
415-344-2000 www.cnetnetworks.com

CNN
One CNN Center/Box 105366, Atlanta, GA 33048
404-827-1700 www.cnn.com

CNN Headline News
One CNN Center/Box 105366, Atlanta, GA 33048
404-827-1700 www.cnn.com/HLN/

Comcast Sports Net
7700 Washington Avenue, Suite 200, Bethesda, MD 20814
301-718-3200 www.comcastsportsnet.com

Comedy Central
1775 Broadway, New York, NY 10019
212-767-8600 www.comedycentral.com

Court TV
600 3rd Avenue, New York, NY 10016
800-COURT-56 www.courttv.com

C-Span 1, 2, 3
400 North Capitol Street NW, Suite 650, Washington, D.C. 20001
202-737-3220 www.c-span.org

CSTV / College Sports Television
Chelsea Piers, Pier 62, New York, NY 10011
212-342-8700 www.cstv.com

The CW Network
4000 Warner Boulevard, Burbank, CA 91522
818-977-5000 www.cwtv.com

DayStar Television Network / DTN
P.O. Box 612066, Dallas, TX 75261
817-571-1229 ww2.daystar.com/Daystar

Discovery (Health, Wings, Science, Times, Home, Kids, Military Channel & FitTV)
7700 Wisconsin Avenue, Bethesda, MD 20814
301-986-1999 www.discovery.com

Disney Channel
3800 West Alameda Avenue, Burbank, CA 91505
818-569-7500 www.disneychannel.com

DIY / Do It Yourself Network
9721 Sherrill Boulevard, Knoxville, TN 37932
865-694-2700 www.diynetwork.com

E! Television
5670 Wilshire Boulevard, Los Angeles, CA 90036
323-692-4815 www.eonline.com

Encore & Encore Westerns
8900 Liberty Circle, Englewood, CO 80112
720-852-7700 www.starz.com

ESPN / ESPN2 / ESPNEWS / ESPN Classic
ESPN Plaza, Bristol, CT 06010
860-766-2000 www.espn.com

EWTN / Eternal World Television Network
5817 Old Leeds Road, Birmingham, AL 35210
205-271-2900 www.ewtn.com

EXPO Communications TV
212-905-8951 www.expotv.com

Fine Living Network
5757 Wilshire Boulevard, Los Angeles, CA 90036
865-694-2700 www.fineliving.com

FitTV
7700 Wisconsin Avenue, Bethesda, MD 20814
301-986-1999 www.fit.discovery.com

FLIX Movie Network
1633 Broadway, New York, NY 10019
800-422-9000 www.show.com

Food Network
1177 Avenue of the Americas, New York, NY 10036
212-398-8836 www.foodtv.com

Fox
2121 Avenue of the Stars, Los Angeles, CA 90067
310-369-2000 www.fox.com

Fox Movie Channel
1440 South Sepulveda, Los Angeles, CA 90025
310-369-2000 www.thefoxmoviechannel.com

Fox News
1211 Avenue of the Americas, New York, NY 10036
888-369-4762 www.foxnews.com

Fox Reality
2121 Avenue of the Stars, Los Angeles, CA 90067
310-369-2000 www.foxreality.com

Fox Sports Net / Sports World / FSW Espanol
10201 West Pico Boulevard, Bldg. 101, Los Angeles, CA 90035
310-369-1000 www.foxsports.com

Fuse TV
11 Penn Plaza, 15th Floor, New York, NY 10001
212-324-3400 www.fuse.tv

FX Network
1000 Santa Monica Boulevard, Los Angeles, CA 90067
310-286-3800 www.fxnetworks.com

G4TechTV
12312 West Olympic Boulevard, Los Angeles, CA 90064
310-979-5100 www.g4techtv.com

GAC / Great American Country
9697 East Mineral Avenue, Englewood, CO 80112
303-792-3111 www.gactv.com

Galavision
9405 NW 41st Street, Miami, FL 33178
305-471-3900 www.galavision.com

GSN / Game Show Network
10202 West Washington Boulevard, West Culver City, CA 90232
310-244-2222 www.gsn.com

The Golf Channel
7580 Commerce Center Drive, Orlando, FL 32819
407-363-4653 www.thegolfchannel.com

Hallmark Channel
12700 Ventura Boulevard, Suite 200, Studio City, CA 91604
888-390-7474 www.hallmarkchannel.com

HBO / HBO Family / HBO Signature
2049 Century Park East, Suite 3600, Los Angeles, CA 90067
310-201-9200 www.hbo.com

HBO—New York
1100 Avenue of the Americas, New York, NY 10036
212-512-1208 www.hbo.com

HDNet
2400 North Ulster Street, Denver, CO 80238
303-542-5600 www.hd.net

HGTV / Home Garden Television
P.O. Box 50970, Knoxville, TN 37950
865-694-7879 www.hgtv.com

History Channel
235 East 45th Street, New York, NY 10017
212-210-1340 www.historychannel.com

Home Shopping Network / HSN
1 HSN Drive, St. Petersburg, FL 33729
800-284-3100 www.hsn.com

i / ion Media Network(formerly PAX TV)
601 Clearwater Park Road, West Palm Beach, FL 33401
561-682-4267 www.ionline.tv

IFC / Independent Film Channel
15 Crossways Park, West Woodbury, NY 11797
516-364-2222 www.ifctv.com

InHD Networks
345 Hudson Street, 17th Floor, New York, NY 10014
646-638-8200 www.inhd.com

Jewelry Television
10001 Kingston Pike, Knoxville, TN 37922
865-692-6000 www.jewelrytelevision.com

Jewish TV
13743 Ventura Boulevard, Suite 200, Sherman Oaks, CA 91423
818-789-5891 www.jewishtvnetwork.com

LATV
2323 Corinth Avenue, Los Angeles, CA 90064
310-943-LATV www.latv.com

TLC / The Learning Channel
7700 Wisconsin Avenue, Bethesda, MD 20814
888-404-5969 www.tlc.discovery.com

Lifetime / Lifetime Movie Network / Life Time Real Women
Worldwide Plaza—309 West 49th Street, New York, NY 10019
212-424-7000 www.lifetimetv.com

LOGO Channel—East
1775 Broadway, 11th Floor, New York, NY 10019
212-258-7800 / 7819 www.logo-tv.com

MBC / MBC News / Major Broadcasting Cable
800 Forrest Street NW, Atlanta, GA 30318
404-350-2509 www.mbcnetwork.com

MSG / Madison Square Garden
2 Pennsylvania Plaza, New York, NY 10021
212-465-6000 www.msgnetwork.com

MSNBC
1 MSNBC Plaza, Secaucus, NJ 07024
888-676-2287 www.msnbc.com

MTV / MTV 2
1515 Broadway, New York, NY 10036
212-258-6000 www.mtv.com/ www.mtv2.com

mun2 (owned by Telemundo)
2470 West 8th Avenue, Hialeah, FL 33010
305-889-7202 www.mun2television.com

National Geographic Channel
1145 17th Street NW, Washington, D.C. 20036
202-912-6500 www.nationalgeographic.com/channel

NBA TV
Olympic Tower—645 Fifth Avenue, New York, NY 10022
212-759-3507 www.nba.com/nba_tv/

NBC
30 Rockefeller Plaza, 25th Floor, Rm 1802, New York, NY 10021
212-664-8046 www.nbc.com

NBC News
30 Rockefeller Plaza, 25th Floor, Rm 1802, New York, NY 10021
212-664-8046 www.nbcnews.com

NewsWorld International (c/o USA Cable)
1230 Avenue of the Americas, New York, NY 10020
212-413-5150 www.nwitv.com

NFL Network / NFL Films
280 Park Avenue, New York, NY 10017
212-450-0040 www.nfl.com/nflnetwork

Nickelodeon
1515 Broadway, New York, NY 10036
212-258-7500 www.nick.com

Noggin / The N
1515 Broadway, New York, NY 10036
212-258-7579 www.noggin.com

OLN / Outdoor Life Network
2 Stanford Plaza, 9th Floor, 281 Tresser Boulevard, Stamford, CT 06901
203-406-2500 www.olntv.com

OTB / Off Track Betting
510 Smith Street, Schenectady, NY 12305
518-344-5226 www.capitalotb.com

The Outdoor Channel
43445 Business Park Drive, Suite 103 Temecula, CA 92950
909-699-6991 www.outdoorchannel.com

Ovation
5801 Duke Street, Suite D, Alexandria, VA 22314
800-Ovation www.ovationtv.com

Oxygen
75 Ninth Avenue, New York, NY 10011
212-651-2000 / 323-860-3500 www.oxygen.com

PBS / Public Broadcast Television
1320 Braddock Place, Alexandria, VA 22314
703-739-5000 www.pbs.com

Playboy TV
2706 Media Center Drive, Los Angeles, CA 90065
323-276-4000 www.playboy.com/playboytv

QVC
1365 Enterprise Drive, West Chester, PA 19380
610-701-1000 www.qvc.com

Rainbow Media Holdings
200 Jericho Quadrangle, Jericho, NY 11723
516-803-3000 www.rainbow-media.com

Realtiy TV USA
240 Center Street, El Segundo, CA 90266
310-356-4843 www.realitytvusa.com

RTN
4175 Cameron Street, Suite B-10, Las Vegas, NV 89103
866-273-3726 www.rtn.tv

The Science Channel
7700 Wisconsin Avenue, Bethesda, MD 20814
301-986-1999 http://science.discovery.com

Sci-Fi Channel
1230 Avenue of the Americas, New York, NY 10020
212-708-7302 www.scifi.com

ShopNBC
6740 Shady Oak Road, Eden Prairie, MN 55344
800-676-5523 www.shopnbc.com

Showtime
1633 Broadway, New York, NY 10019
212-708-7302 www.sho.com

SNY / SportsNet New York (Mets/Jets)
75 Rockefeller Plaza, New York, NY 10019
212-485-4800 www.sny.tv

SoapNET
3800 West Alameda Avenue, Burbank, CA 91505
818-569-3333 http://soapnet.go.com

Speed Channel
9711 Southern Pine Boulevard, Charlotte, NC 28273
704-731-2222 www.speedtv.com

Spike TV
1515 Broadway, New York, NY 10036
212-846-4095 www.spiketv.com

Starz
8900 Liberty Circle, Englewood, CO 80112
720-852-7700 www.starz.com

Style Network
5670 Wilshire Boulevard, Los Angeles, CA 90036
323-954-2400 www.stylenetwork.com

Sun Sports
> 1000 Legion Place, Suite 1600, Orlando, FL 32801
> 407-648-1150 www.sunsportstv.com

Sundance Channel
> 1633 Broadway, 14th Floor, New York, NY 10019
> 212-708-1600 www.sundancechannel.com

TBN / Trinity Broadcast Network
> 2424 Michelle, Tustin, CA 92789
> 714-832-2950 www.tbn.org

TBS
> One CNN Center, Atlanta, GA 30348
> 404-885-4488 www.tbs.com

TCM / The Movie Channel
> 1050 Techwood Drive, Atlanta, GA 30318
> 404-885-5535 www.turnerclassicmovies.com

Telemundo Network
> 2470 West 8th Avenue, Hialeah, FL 33010
> 305-884-8200 www.telmundo.com

The Tennis Channel
> 2850 Ocean Park Boulvard, Santa Monica, CA 90405
> 310-314-9400 www.thetennischannel.com

TLC / The Learning Channel
> 7700 Wisconsin Avenue, Bethesda, MD 20814
> 888-404-5969 www.tlc-discovery.com

TNT
> 1050 Techwood Drive, Atlanta, GA 30318
> 404-885-4538 www.tnt.tv

TOON Disney Channel
> 3800 West Alameda Avenue, Burbank, CA 91505
> 818-569-7500 http://psc.disney.go.com/abcnetworks/toondisney

Travel Channel
> 7770 Wisconsin Avenue, Bethesda, MD 20814
> 888-404-5969 www.travel.discovery.com

TV Asia / Asia Star Broadcasting, Inc.
> 76 National Road, Edison, NJ 08817
> 732-650-1100 www.tvasiausa.com

TV Guide Channel
>   6922 Hollywood Boulevard, Los Angeles, CA 90028
>   323-817-4899   www.tvguideinc.com

TVG / The Interactive Horseracing Network
>   19545 NW Von Neumann Drive, Suite 210, Beaverton, OR 97006
>   888-PLAY-TVG   www.tvg.com

TV Land
>   1515 Broadway, New York, NY 10036
>   212-258-7500   www.nickatnite.com

Univision
>   9405 NW 41st, Miami, FL 33178
>   305-471-3900   www.univision.com

USA Networks
>   1230 Avenue of the Americas, 3rd Floor, New York, NY 10020
>   212-314-7300   www.usanetworks.com

VH-1 / VH-1 Classics
>   1515 Broadway, New York, NY 10036
>   212-258-7500   www.vh1.com

WAM! (owned by Encore)
>   5445 DTC Parkway, Suite 600, Englewood, CO 80111
>   303-771-7700   www.encoretv.com

The Weather Channel
>   300 Interstate Parkway, Atlanta, GA 30339
>   770-226-0000   www.weather.com

We / Women's Entertainment
>   150 Crossways Park West, Woodbury, NY 11797
>   516-396-3000   www.we-womensentertainment.com

WGM
>   2501 West Bradley Place, Chicago, IL 60618
>   773-528-2311   www.wgncable.com

Wisdom Channel
>   P.O. Box 1546, Bluefield, WV 24701
>   304-323-8000   www.wisdommedia.com

The Word Network
>   20733 West Ten Mile, Southfield, MI 48075
>   248-357-4566   www.thewordnetwork.com

VOA / Voice of America
Office of Public Affairs
330 Independence Avenue, SW Washington, D.C. 20237
202-203-4959/ www.voanews.com

Yes Network
405 Lexington Avenue, 36th Floor, New York, NY 10174
646-487-3600 www.yesnetwork.com

Zee TV
1615 W Abram, Suite 200C, Arlington, TX 76013
817-274-2933 www.zeetelevision.com

Daytime Talk Shows

Dr. Phil **/ Paramount Studios**
860 North Gower Street, Hollywood, CA 90028
www.drphil.com
Type: Relationship

The Ellen Degeneres Show **/ Telepictures Productions**
3000 West Alameda Avenue, Burbank, CA 91523
www.ellen.warnerbros.com
Type: Variety

Jerry Springer **/ NBC Universal**
454 North Columbus Drive, 2nd Floor, Chicago, IL 60611
www.jerryspringertv.com
Type: Relationship

Live with Regis and Kelly **/ Buena Vista Television**
7 Lincoln Square, New York, NY 10023
ttp://tvplex.go.com/buenavista/regisandkelly
Type: Variety

The Martha Stewart Show **/ NBC Universal**
220 West 26th Street, New York, NY 10011
www.marthastewart.com/martha
Type: Lifestyle

The Maury Povich Show **/ NBC Universal**
15 Penn Plaza/Grand Ballroom, New York, New York 10001
www.mauryshow.com
Type: Relationship

The Montel Williams Show / **Paramount**
    433 West 53rd Street, New York, NY 10019
    www.montelshow.com
    Type: Relationship

The Morning Show with Mike and Juliet / **Twentieth Television**
    2121 Avenue of the Stars, 21st floor, Los Angeles, CA 90067
    www.mandjshow.com
    Type: Talk/Variety

The Oprah Winfrey Show / **Harpo Productions**
    1058 West Washington, Chicago, IL 60607
    www.oprah.com
    Type: Relationship

The Rachael Ray Show / **Harpo Productions/Paramount Television**
    222 East 44th Street at Screen Gems Studios, New York, NY 10017
    http://www.rachaelrayshow.com/
    Type: Lifestyle

The Tyra Banks Show / **Telepictures Productions**
    7800 Beverly Boulevard, Los Angeles, CA 90036
    http://tyrashow.warnerbros.com
    Type: Relationship

The View / **ABC Daytime and Barwall Productions**
    7 West 66th Street, New York, NY 10023
    http://abc.go.com/daytime/theview/
    Type: Variety

News and Entertainment Shows

Access Hollywood / **NBC Universal**
    www.accesshollywood.com
    Type: Entertainment News

American Morning / **CNN**
    1271 Avenue of the Americas, New York, NY 10020
    http://www.cnn.com/CNN/Programs/american.morning/
    Type: Cable Morning News

The Early Show / CBS News
51 West 52nd Street, Suite 35, New York, NY 10019
http://www.cbsnews.com/sections/earlyshow/main500202.shtml
Type: Morning News

Entertainment Tonight / Paramount Television
http://et.tv.yahoo.com
Type: Entertainment News

Extra / Warner Bros. Television
http://extratv.warnerbros.com
Type: Entertainment News

Fox & Friends / FOX News
1211 Avenue of the Americas, New York, NY 10036
http://www.foxnews.com/foxfriends/index.html
Type: Cable Morning News

Good Morning America / ABC News
7 West 66th Street, New York, NY 10023
http://abcnews.go.com/GMA/
Type: Morning News

Inside Edition / King World Productions
www.insideedition.com
Type: Entertainment News

The Insider / Paramount Television
http://insider.tv.yahoo.com
Type: Entertainment News

Today / NBC News
30 Rockefeller Plaza, New York, NY 10112
http://www.msnbc.msn.com/id/3032633/
Type: Morning News

Nighttime Talk Shows

The Daily Show with Jon Stewart
513 West 54th Street, New York, NY 10019
http://www.comedycentral.com/shows/the_daily_show/index.jhtml
Type: Variety

Jimmy Kimmel Live / **El Capitan Entertainment Center**
    6840 Hollywood Boulevard, Hollywood, CA 90028
    http://abc.go.com/primetime/jimmykimmel/index.html
    Type: Variety

Last Call with Carson Daly / **NBC Studios (Stage 9)**
    3000 West Alameda Avenue, Burbank, CA 91523
    http://www.nbc.com/Last_Call_with_Carson_Daly/
    Type: Variety

The Late Late Show with Craig Fergurson / **Worldwide Pants**
    1697 Broadway, Suite 805, New York, NY 10019
    http://www.cbs.com/latenight/latelate/
    Type: Variety

Late Night with Conan O'Brien
    30 Rockefeller Plaza, New York, NY 10112
    http://www.nbc.com/Late_Night_with_Conan_O'Brien/index.shtml
    Type: Variety

Late Show with David Letterman / **Worldwide Pants**
    1697 Broadway, Suite 805, New York, NY 10019
    http://www.cbs.com/latenight/lateshow/
    Type: Variety

The Tonight Show with Jay Leno / **NBC Universal**
    3000 West Alameda Avenue, West Burbank, CA 91523
    http://www.nbc.com/The_Tonight_Show_with_Jay_Leno/
    Type: Variety